Communications
in Computer and Information Science   1002

Commenced Publication in 2007
Founding and Former Series Editors:
Phoebe Chen, Alfredo Cuzzocrea, Xiaoyong Du, Orhun Kara, Ting Liu,
Krishna M. Sivalingam, Dominik Ślęzak, and Xiaokang Yang

Editorial Board Members

More information about this series at http://www.springer.com/series/7899

Habib M. Fardoun · Ahlam A. M. Hassan ·
M. Elena de la Guía (Eds.)

New Technologies to Improve Patient Rehabilitation

4th Workshop, REHAB 2016
Lisbon, Portugal, October 13–14, 2016
Revised Selected Papers

 Springer

Editors
Habib M. Fardoun (iD)
King Abdulaziz University
Jeddah, Saudi Arabia

M. Elena de la Guía (iD)
Computer Science Research Institute
University of Castilla-La Mancha
Albacete, Spain

Ahlam A. M. Hassan
Center for Accreditation and Quality
Ahlia University
Manama, Bahrain

ISSN 1865-0929   ISSN 1865-0937 (electronic)
Communications in Computer and Information Science
ISBN 978-3-030-16784-4   ISBN 978-3-030-16785-1 (eBook)
https://doi.org/10.1007/978-3-030-16785-1

Library of Congress Control Number: 2019936146

This Springer imprint is published by the registered company Springer Nature Switzerland AG
The registered company address is: Gewerbestrasse 11, 6330 Cham, Switzerland

Preface

During the past few years, there has been increasing interest in the application of virtual reality and information and communication technologies (ICTs) in the field of rehabilitation, with clinical results that prove their effectiveness.

New technologies such as Kinect, virtual reality, sensors, augmented reality, eye tracking, 3D printers, etc. allow us to develop innovative solutions for assistance, prevention, and rehabilitation in patients. In this way, the new technologies can help patients to function more easily in their everyday lives and can also make it easier for a caregiver to care them.

The main focus of this book titled *New Technologies to Improve Patient Rehabilitation* is to explore how technology can contribute toward smarter and effective rehabilitation methods. Contained herein are ten chapters:

Chapter 1 analyzes the effects of extrinsic feedback together with virtual system in children with cerebral palsy. Chapter 2 evaluates whether the motor rehabilitation and treatment of cognitive symptoms could have a synergistic contribution to the recovery of the patient after stroke. Chapter 3 describes and evaluates an EMG-based approach for estimating the joint angles of the fingers and wrist. The proposed approach utilizes the discrete wavelet transform (DWT) to analyze the EMG signals in the time-frequency domain. Chapter 4 presents and evaluates some proposals based on 3D rehabilitation games for neural rehabilitation; the main idea is helping patients to recover their mobility, which was lost via a neurological accident, or to confront their phobia. Chapter 5 examines the basic psychomotor deficits of individuals with hearing impairment (HI) and reviews the literature to compile systems that help train and improve their psychomotor skills, and then proposes some interactive systems. Chapter 6 presents a methodology for gait identification using the on-board sensors of a smart rollator: the i-Walker. This technique provides the number of steps taken in walking exercises, as well as the time and distance travelled for each stride. Chapter 7 describes the design and implementation of a simple and cost-effective health-care monitoring and fall detection system that utilizes of-the-shelf electronic components. The system consists of a microcontroller, medical sensors, and communication module that are used to collect patients' information and send it to the cloud for further processing and analysis. Chapter 8 reports the results of an original mixed-methods survey on the experiences and attitudes of disabled people toward digital games in rehabilitation. Chapter 9 presents a study that examines how the number of pages in the informed consent (IC) influences reading behavior. Chapter 10 reports on a study that examines the value of several common usability testing protocols, methods, and metrics when used to evaluate the usability of a new personalized reminiscence 'app' called InspireD. InspireD is a bespoke app designed to support personalized reminiscence for people living with dementia.

Finally, we would like to thank all authors for the valuable contributions presented, all the organizers (King Abdulaziz University, Ahlia University, Bahrain and ISE

Research group UCLM) and collaborators (COPELABS, Lusophone University, Lisbon, Portugal), together with the reviewers (members of the Program Committee) for helping us by contributing to a high-quality book on the topics of rehabilitation.

November 2018   Habib M. Fardoun
                                                    Ahlam A. M. Hassan
                                             M. Elena de la Guía

Organization

King Abdulaziz University, Ahlia University, Bahrain, and ISE Research group (UCLM)

Chairs and Program Co-chairs

Habib M. Fardoun   King Abdulaziz University, Saudi Arabia
Ahlam A. M. Hassan   Ahlia University, Bahrain
Elena de la Guía   University of Castilla-La Mancha, Spain

Organizing Committee

Pedro Gamito   Lusophone University, Portugal
Sergio Albiol Pérez   University of Zaragoza, Spain
Victor M. R. Penichet   University of Castilla-La Mancha, Spain
Daniyal M. Alghazzawi   King Abdulaziz University, Saudi Arabia

Program Committee

Belinda Lange   Institute for Creative Technologies,
    University of Southern California, USA
Willem-Paul Brinkman   Delft University of Technology, The Netherlands
Mariano Luis Alcañiz   Instituto Interuniversitario de Investigación
    en Bioingeniería, Spain
Beatriz Rey   Universidad Politécnica de Valencia, Spain
Imre Cikajlo   Univerzitetni rehabilitacijski inštitut Republike
    Slovenije, Slovenia
Roberto Lloréns   Instituto Interuniversitario de Investigación
    en Bioingeniería, Spain
José Antonio Gil   Universidad Politécnica de Valencia, Spain
Mónica Cameirão   University of Madeira, Portugal
Sergi Bermudez   University of Madeira, Portugal
Emily Keshner   Temple University, USA
Hermenegildo Gil   Universidad Politécnica de Valencia, Spain
Kjartan Halvorsen   Uppsala University, Sweden
Thalmann Daniel   University of Paul Sabatier, France
Rosa Maria E. Moreira   Universidade do Estado do Rio de Janeiro, Brazil
Georgina Cárdenas-López   Universidad Nacional Autónoma de México, Mexico
Evelyne Klinger   French National Research Agency, France
Ben Challis   Cardiff School of Creative and Cultural Industries, UK
Guillermo Palacios   University of Zaragoza, Spain

Rachel Proffitt	University of Southern California, USA
Jaime Sánchez	University of Chile, Chile
Félix Albertos Marco	ISE Research Group, UCLM, Spain
Gregor Wolbring	University of Calgary, Canada
Maria Elisa Pimentel Piemonte	University of São Paulo, Brazil
Ala Khalifeh	German Jordanian University, Jordan
Jose Eduardo Pompeu	Federal University of São Paulo, Brazil
Rosa Costa	UERJ, Brazil
Giuseppe Depietro	ICAR CNR (Italian National Council of Research), Italy
María Dolores Lozano	Universidad de Castilla-La Mancha, Spain
José Antonio Gallud Lazaro	Universidad de Castilla-La Mancha, Spain
Ricardo Tesoriero	Universidad de Castilla-La Mancha, Spain
Christos Bouras	University of Patras and RACTI, Greece

Contents

Effects of Extrinsic Feedback in Virtual Rehabilitation for Children with Cerebral Palsy: A Comprehensive Systematic Review

Nancy Jacho-Guanoluisa[1(✉)], Sergio Albiol-Pérez[2] (iD),
Sonsoles Valdivia-Salas[2], Ricardo Jariod-Gaudes[3],
Cesar A. Collazos[4] (iD), and Habib M. Fardoun[5] (iD)

[1] Universidad de las Fuerzas Armadas ESPE, Sangolquí, Ecuador
npjacho@espe.edu.ec
[2] Aragón Health Research Institute (IIS Aragón),
Universidad de Zaragoza, Teruel, Spain
{salbiol, sonsoval}@unizar.es
[3] Aragón Health Research Institute (IIS Aragón),
H.U. Miguel Servet, Zaragoza, Spain
rjariod@salud.aragon.es
[4] Systems Program, University of Cauca, Popayan, Colombia
ccollazo@unicauca.edu.co
[5] Teaching Excellence Department, Ahlia University, Bahrain Systems,
Manama, Bahrain
hfardonn@ahlia.edu.bh

Abstract. Children with Cerebral Palsy (CP) have motor and cognitive disorders that make it difficult for them to perform activities of daily living (ADL). Virtual Rehabilitation (VR) is a relatively novel research line that tackles motor and cognitive abilities. Sensory feedback together with Virtual Environments (VE) enriches and improves motor control in children with CP. The use of VR together with intrinsic/extrinsic feedback in intervention periods is a complement of training sessions with clear and relevant outcomes. In this paper, we analyze the effects of extrinsic feedback together with virtual systems in children with CP. An exhaustive literature search was carried out in electronic databases, from 2008 to 2018 to identify studies. The American Academy for Cerebral Palsy and Developmental Medicine (AACPDM) systematic review methodology was used as a frame-work. Outcomes reveal improvements in gait, stride length, walking speed, and stride time by using extrinsic feedback. Future research should be focused on the design and validation of the these system with larger groups of children with CP.

Keywords: Virtual reality · Feedback · Cerebral Palsy ·
Human computer interaction · Virtual Rehabilitation

© Springer Nature Switzerland AG 2019
H. M. Fardoun et al. (Eds.): REHAB 2016, CCIS 1002, pp. 1–13, 2019.
https://doi.org/10.1007/978-3-030-16785-1_1

1 Introduction

Cerebral Palsy (CP) is a set of disorders that causes motor alterations and deficits in postural control and balance [1, 2]. Patients with CP show cognitive and motor impairments as well [3]. In recent years, the prevalence of CP has increased to 2.11 per 1,000 subjects in developed countries [4]. CP can be sub-classified in different types of motor disturbances: (1) monoplegia; (2) hemiplegia; (3) diplegia; and (4) quadriplegia. Spastic hemiplegia and the diplegia are the most prevalent [2] in children with CP.

Motor function of children and young people with CP can be categorized into five levels, according to the Gross Motor Function Classification System (GMFCS) [5]. Level-I includes children with CP who can perform all the activities of their age-matched peers, with limited speed, balance, and coordination. Level V includes children with CP who have difficulties in postural control of the head, trunk, and involuntary movements [5].

Physical therapies in rehabilitation processes of children with CP show improvements in motor and cognitive disorders thanks to the use of customizable VR training programs [6]. Neurorehabilitation services for children, hospitals and center-based child care are incorporating the use of Virtual Systems as a tool to enrich traditional physical therapies for children with CP [6–8]. Interactive environments simulated through VR allow practicing and testing novel alternatives in a planned and secure environment. VR enriches personal control, including motor skills [9], or self-efficacy in patients, increasing their self- esteem [10] as a consequence.

VR feedback is the information provided to perform correct movements, during or after training sessions, to show improvements with respect to previous established goals [11]. VR feedback engages patients thus facilitating the improvement of motor functionality [12]. Such is the case that VR feedback is considered to increase motivation [13] and adherence to treatment, enriching therapeutic sessions [14]. Specifically, the use of VR feedback is a novel option to enrich motor learning [15].

Feedback can be classified as 'intrinsic' or 'extrinsic'. Intrinsic feedback is sensory-perceptual information obtained during the execution of a task [16]. Intrinsic feedback stimulates and activates the mechanoreceptors of skin, which, as a result, causes improvements in patients with sensory alterations [17].

Extrinsic feedback is a complement of intrinsic feedback and can be run concurrently while performing the task. Extrinsic feedback shows information related to movements, and can be shown in a verbal form (words) or a non-verbal form (auditory-visual) or haptic, depending on what most appropriate to the movements target of the treatment [12]. While extrinsic visual feedback helps patients understand their movements and carry out compensatory strategies according to the correct motor exercises [18, 19], extrinsic auditory feedback contributes to a more precise motor control in therapeutic sessions [20]. Extrinsic haptic feedback can be classified into two categories. On the one hand, the forceful feedback, that makes use of the weight of the virtual objects and the force applied in the muscles and joints of the subject with CP to fulfill the movement. On the other hand, the tactile sensation that allows the user to feel the roughness of virtual surfaces (textures), edges (shapes) and temperature [21, 22].

Interactive feedback systems in VR provide tracking systems together with visual, auditory, and haptic feedback. Interactive feedback systems offer detailed information of advances in the intervention and follow-up periods. It has been shown their efficacy to reduce motor impairment [23].

In this paper, we carry out a systematic review of the results obtained after a VR program that incorporates extrinsic feedback techniques for the rehabilitation of motor functions of children presenting CP.

2 Methods

This review was performed using the AACPDM methodology (revision 1.2) 2008, which was developed to specifically analyze medical treatment outcomes with CP population [24]. AACPDM provides significant Levels of Evidence in Research (LER) and an explicit strategy to examine outcomes together with the International Classification of Functioning (ICF) of Disabilities and Health [25]. We carried out a literature search from January 2008 to August 2018 in the following electronics databases: Pubmed, Scopus and ScienceDirect.

2.1 Inclusion Criteria

To be included in the present article, studies: (1) included children and teenagers under 18 years old presenting with CP; (2) employed VR with extrinsic feedback during the intervention; (3) presented outcomes related to motor control; and (4) were written in English, or translated into English, and published in scientific journals.

2.2 Search Strategy

This review includes studies which included the following keywords: feedback, implicit and explicit feedback, extrinsic feedback (in the field Title), VR, virtual treatment, virtual reality, VE, child, or children (in all fields); and studies that analyze disorders of children with CP. Once the search was conducted, the reference lists of retrieved articles were reviewed to identify potentially relevant articles.

The initial search in electronic databases reported 91 articles. All articles were selected by the title and three additional articles were added through manual search. The abstract of eighty-four articles were reviewed. After excluding 18 articles based on their abstract, 64 articles were examined for eligibility. The excluded studies are described in the PRISMA model [26] (Fig. 1). Finally, 10 studies were selected to analyze the effectiveness of feedback techniques in virtual reality.

2.3 Classification of the Outcomes

AACPDM measures the quality of studies by using a hierarchy of Level of Evidence of Research (LER). This hierarchy is organized by types of studies, and contains the following levels: (1) level I: randomized controlled trials with a number of participants greater than one hundred; (2) level II: randomized controlled trials with a sample size less than one hundred participants; (3) level III: cohort studies; (4) level IV: case reports or cohort studies without a concurrent control group; and (5) level V: studies based on expert opinions, reports, electronic databases focused on research, etc. Level I produce satisfactory and reliable outcomes due to statistical results obtained and based on a high sample size. Level II and Level III inform partial conclusions due to sample size, because this sample has less than one hundred participants, and therefore statistical outcomes are not reliable. From Level IV and Level V it is impossible to get conclusions due to minimum sample size.

AACPDM establishes seven criteria to test for research quality, specifically: (1) Did researchers analyze and correctly describe the inclusion and exclusion criteria of the sample? (2) Were the experimental and control groups described in detail? (3) In regards to the outcomes of interest, were the methods clearly described, valid, and reliable? (4) Were outcomes achieved with a blind evaluation? (5) Was a correct statistical analysis performed? (6) Was dropout rate considered in the study and was it less than 20% of sample size? And (7) did the design include the control of possible confounding variables? [24] Depending on the answer to these questions, a particular study may be classified as having weak, moderate, or strong evidence.

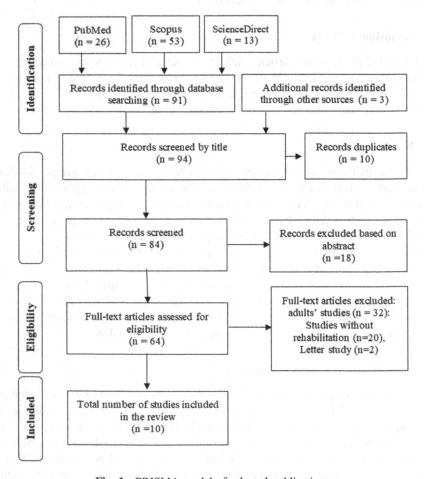

Fig. 1. PRISMA model of selected publications.

AACPDM classifies outcomes using components described in the ICF and components of disability and health of ICF, developed by the World Health Organization [25]. The ICF components of health have three dimensions: (1) body function / body structure, anatomical parts of the body (organs, limbs, and their components), and physiological and psychological functions of body parts and systems; (2) activity in a task and participation to perform an action related to ADL; and (3) environmental factors such as physical, social, technological, and attitudinal [25].

3 Results

A total of 10 studies met the inclusion criteria and were fully reviewed. As can be seen in Table 1, according to the AACPDM, we included: (1) a case report [27], focused on augmented feedback; (2) two case studies focused on haptic feedback by using an interactive humanoid robot combined with a VR System [28, 29]; (3) two studies which compare outcomes of cohort studies with concurrent control groups [30, 31]; (4) four randomized controlled trials with less than one hundred participants [32, 33]; and (5) a study which reports the opinion of clinical experts [34].

Due to quality offered from Level I to Level III of the AACPDM, we finally selected the six papers that appear in Table 2, to do our systematic review.

Table 1. Summary of studies: intervention and participants (group studies)

Year Author Citation	LER Design	Participant (GMFCS)	Total n	Ages	Intervention Protocol	Control intervention
2017 Chen [29]	V Case Study	CP (I y III)	17 EG = 10 CG = 7	8–12 years	Applies two games with SPVR without RD and AF (baseline), three games with SPVR and RD and VF (acquisition) and at the end two games SPVR without RD and ViF (extinction) 75 s with 10 movements Duration: NS	CTS with children TD
2017 Gelder [35]	II Smaller RCT's	SCP (I-III)	27 EG = 16 CG = 11	6–16 years	The children walked on the Gait Real-time Analysis Interactive Lab (GRAIL) with a flexed-knee gait pattern, walked on an instrumented treadmill with VR in three conditions: regular walking without feedback (NF), ViF on hip angle and VF on knee angle 2 min per session Duration = NS	CTS with children TD

(continued)

Table 1. (*continued*)

Year Author Citation	LER Design	Participant (GMFCS)	Total n	Ages	Intervention Protocol	Control intervention
2017 Pu [33]	II Smaller RCT's	SDPC with dynamic equinus (I-II)	13	4–11 years	The three gait tests were as follows: (1) daily gait: Subjects walked naturally; (2) conventional training gait: The monitoring device was muted. Subjects make a conscious effort to "walk with a normal gait"; (3) feedback training gait. AF was turned on when subjects should increase the pressure and duration of heel 2–3 min per session, walking 10 m, next 5-min rest period Duration = NS	Gait CTS with children TD and feedback training gait
2015 Sloot [31]	III Cohort studies	SPC (I or II)	20 EG = 9 CG = 11	8–15 years	Subjects walked independently without aids and wore a safety harness. ViF was applied. Subject saw treadmill placed with 180° projection of straight forest road and scenery Four trials of 3 min were randomly performed: walking at FS and SP, both with and without VR. Last minute of trials was used for analysis Duration = NS	Subject walked 6–10 min to familiarize with self-paced (SP) and fixed speed (FS) treadmill walking. A SP trial was performed to determine the speed and in FS was set
2014 Pu [34]	V Expert Opinion	4 SDCP 4 CHCP	16 EG = 8 CG = 8	2–9 years	Each subject walked 10 steps while wearing the custom-built shoes embedded with intelligent insoles. AF inform that users were abnormal steps. Pressure signals were transmitted to a smartphone via Bluetooth and saved a video of the sagittal plane of user Duration = NS	The same intervention process but with children with TD

(*continued*)

Table 1. (*continued*)

Year Author Citation	LER Design	Participant (GMFCS)	Total n	Ages	Intervention Protocol	Control intervention
2013 López [30]	III Cohort studies	CP (I, II)	15 EG = 9 CG = 8	8–12 years	Task 1, for upper limbs and Task 2, for upper and lower limbs. Three exercises are performed to analyzed abnormal motor patterns of children with CP using ViF 15–20 min and included two tasks, 3 per week Duration = 2 week	The children TD recorded the tasks to extract the coordinates of the correct motor control
2013 Wood [36]	II Smaller RCT	EG = 2 (IV) (I) CG = 4 (IV) (III) (I)	6 EG = 2 EC = 4	5–18 years	The therapist configures the parameters of the direction, the magnitude of the gesture and the delay time for feedback Each subject participated in both conventional and robotic therapy to improve either forearm supination or wrist extension. Robotic therapy used AF and ViF 20 min, 2 per week Duration = 5 week	CTS as first intervention later received robotic therapy and EG subjects received therapy crossover
2012 Baram [32]	II Smaller RCT	EG = CP CG = TD	35 EG1 = 10 CG1 = 7 EG2 = 10 CG2 = 8	6–26 years	In the first week, EG1 and CG1 trained with ViF. In the second week, EG2 and CG2 trained with AF. In the third week, six EG subjects trained with AF and ViF and seven CG subjects trained with ViF and AF 20 min per day Duration = 20 days	Three training programs with different feedbacks

(*continued*)

Table 1. (*continued*)

Year Author Citation	LER Design	Participant (GMFCS)	Total n	Ages	Intervention Protocol	Control intervention
2011 Choi [28]	V Case Study	Subject1, dystonia HPC [37] Subject2, dyskinesia CP (III)	2	7 years	Process A: First week. Participants take a pre-test by writing the 10 test characters without HF and practice handwriting with haptic guidance of both drag force and guiding force Process B was carry out in second week and it was identical to process A. Subject practice handwriting with haptic guidance only of guiding force 30 min, 2 per week Duration = 2 week	Practicing handwriting with full HF (drag force and guiding force) and guiding force feedback
2010 Patritti [27]	IV Case Serie	2 CP [37] 2 CP (III)	4; EG = 2 CG = 2	5–8 years	Gait training using a robotic driven gait orthosis (DGO) One child of each GMFCS level was tested using DGO, while the other child of each pair was tested without the augmented feedback module 30 min, 3 per week Duration = 6 week, 3-month follow-up	One child of each level pair tested without the augmented feedback module

LER, Level of Evidence of Research; EG, Experimental Group; CG, Control Group; CP, Cerebral Palsy; SDICP, Spastic Diplegia Cerebral Palsy; SPC, Spastic Cerebral Palsy; CHCP, Congenital Hemiplegia Cerebral Palsy; SPVR, Super Pop Virtual Reality Game; RD, Robot Darwin; AF, Auditory Feedback; VF, Verbal Feedback; ViF, Visual Feedback; HF, Haptic Feedback; TD, Typically Developing; NS, not specified; RCT, Randomized Controlled Trials; GMFCS, The Gross Motor Function Classification; CTS, Conventional Training Session.

Table 2. Conduct ratings of studies ranging from Level I to Level III.

Study	Example	1	2	3	4	5	6	7
2012 Baram [32]	II Weak	No	Yes	No	Yes	Yes	No	No
2013 López [30]	II Weak	Yes	No	No	No	No	No	Yes
2015 Sloot [31]	II Weak	Yes	No	Yes	No	No	No	Yes
2016 Wood [36]	II Moderate	Yes	Yes	Yes	Yes	No	No	No
2017 Gelder [35]	II Moderate	Yes	Yes	Yes	Yes	No	Yes	No
2017 Pu [33]	II Moderate	Yes	Yes	Yes	No	Yes	Yes	Yes

4   Discussion

Several research groups have been working with VR systems for upper extremity [36], lower extremity [31–33], upper and lower extremity [30] and other body parts [35] of children with CP as novel rehabilitation modalities.

Overall, VR systems with extrinsic feedback improve and enrich mobility in patients with gait, forearm supination/pronation, trunk, and hip disorders. Visual and auditory feedback alleviates motor impairment in children with CP, hence improving his/her quality of life.

4.1   Body Functions/Body Structure

Movement Functions in Lower Limbs. Findings from three studies [31–33, 36] demonstrate that extrinsic feedback improves the motor function of lower limbs in children with CP.

Sloot et al. [31] modified the gait pattern in TD and CP children (GMFCS Level I or II). Visual feedback-controlled treadmills with a VE allowed subjects to increase walking speed and its between-stride variability. Walking with treadmills with a VE was similar to overground walking and showed no relevant effects on kinematic or kinetic parameters. The results showed problems of integration between study groups, showing that children with CP might need more time to become familiar with the walk. Visual feedback allowed creating a very similar motivational environment as when walking on the ground.

Baram et al. [32] analyzed the improvement of gait in children with SPC after using auditory and visual feedback to train walking speed and stride length along a 10 m straight track. Results showed that visual feedback improved the performance of lower extremities. Patients with CP of older age showed higher improvement after training with auditory and visual feedback. Healthy controls subjects left little room for improvement.

Pu et al. [33] examined how real-time feedback impacts walking performance during gait training. Outcomes showed that auditory feedback produced improvement in toe-walking gait. This contributed to improve motor control of lower limb through lengthening tight muscles, stretching tendons and increasing joint's range of motion. This feedback encouraged patients with CP (GMFCS = I, II) to increase heel loading pressure and duration in each stride to improve physiological gait.

Movement Functions in Upper Limbs. Wood et al. [36] worked with children with CP (Spastic Quadriplegia, Spastic Left Hemiplegia, Athetoid Quadriplegia, Spastic Right Hemiplegia) with different GMFCS level, and demonstrated slight differences between conventional therapy and robotic therapy with visual and auditory feedback in the improvement of forearm supination/pronation or wrist extension/flexion function. The reasons were: (1) patient's group was heterogeneous and small; (2) robotic system provided feedback to subject very quickly. Use of a robotic feedback system improved movement in the targeted gesture when robotic feedback therapy intervention was applied before conventional therapy intervention [36].

Movement Functions in Upper and Lower Limbs. López et al. [30] analyzed motor learning in children with CP (GMFCS = I, II) by providing feedback in a VR system with the purpose of improving abnormal movements. Tasks included three movements for the evaluation of each type of limb. Participants performed exercises related to dancing and the system analyzed abnormal motor patterns in upper and lower limbs. Visual feedback improved learning of pronation and supination movements of the upper limbs.

Movement Functions in Other Parts of the Body. Gelder et al. [35] analyzed if children with CP (GMFCS I-III) can adapt their gait in response to real-time feedback by using kinematic parameters. To test for this hypothesis, children with CP walked with a flexed-knee gait pattern on a treadmill with an immersive semicircular screen in three conditions: walking without feedback, feedback on the hip angle, and feedback on the knee angle. Visual feedback in this study provide the following outcomes: (1) improvements in trunk kinematics (position) and movements; (2) improvements in the extension of hip and knee, adapting the speed of walking; (3) no significant differences were found in the spasticity results because they are not functional measures. Outcomes showed, that children with CP adapted gait and were able to respond to visual real-time feedback, focusing their attention on the task.

Strength and Muscle Tone Functions. Pu et al. [33] showed that auditory feedback incorporated in sensorized insoles increased children attention to heel loading pressure and duration. These allowed activation of muscle stretching, changing the biomechanical properties of the tendon of the calf muscle and improving motor control.

4.2 Environmental Factors

Physical, social and technological factors are considered environmental factors. Overall, VR system together with extrinsic feedback improves mobility of children with CP.

Technology Systems. VR environments that use only visual feedback have contributed: (1) to slightly improve gait speed (by using a walking belt equipped with a double strap and 180 projection landscapes) [31]; (2) to improve learning of the pronation and supination (by using an optical motion tracking system that captures reference points of the child's body) [30]; (3) to enrich peak hip and knee extension impairments (by using an belt integrated in the treadmill [35].

VE that use visual and auditory feedback improve walking speed, stride length [32], and forearm pronation/supination or wrist extension/flexion [36], by using different technology. In Baram et al. [32], visual feedback was shown at a display that was attached to the eyeglasses frame, providing patients with images of their own motion. Auditory feedback (a click) in response to each step was provided via earphones. Both devices included an inertial motion sensor and a computing unit integrated in a belt-mounted box. In Wood et al. [36], CosmoBot system was designed to provide time real feedback and to improve forearm supination/pronation or wrist extension/flexion motion. Robot movements provided immediate feedback to the child about the attempted movement. Three-dimensional movement data were collected at a frequency of 60 Hz using a 10 camera high-resolution optical motion capture system. Kinematics were calculated in Visual3D and Mathlab [36].

Pu et al. [33] employed a VE together with auditory feedback and showed increases in heel loading percentage and corrected toe-walking gait. This study used a monitored toe-walking gait feedback system based on the dynamic heel pressure index (DFPI) with an auditory stimulus warning when steps were abnormal or without adequate heel pressure [33]. A customizable environment was designed for different feet and was adjusted to a circuit board to store plantar pressure. A smartphone collected experimental data and analyzed normal/abnormal strides length [33].

4.3 Other Components

According to AACPDM methodology, Level IV and Level V contain too much bias to draw firm conclusions. Studies within these categories, however, provide interesting information to be considered. We briefly review here the four articles which were excluded from our systematic review. Chen et al. [29] showed that, through the use of a socially interactive humanoid robot, children with and without CP can improve their movements even after the feedback is removed. Choi et al. [28] employed hand haptic rehabilitation which improved the handwriting ability of children with CP. Patritti et al. [27] showed that visual, auditory and haptic feedback improves walking function and speed. In Pu et al. [34], a feedback system based on plantar pressure was developed to detect toe-walking strides. It produced a sound to inform user when abnormal strides were encountered.

5 Conclusions

At the level of body functions, extrinsic feedback by using devices such as treadmills with immersive semicircular, sensorized insoles, and robots, improved performance in children with CP (GMFCS I, II and III).

There are several limitations that should be considered in this review: limited number of subjects in each study. In the selected studies, participants were classified in different levels of GMFCS and it was difficult to analyze the outcomes due to the heterogeneity of the sample. No studies have used psychometrically valid measures to assess motion rehabilitation in children with CP in levels IV and V of GMFCS.

At the level of environmental factors, technology used to provide visual and auditory feedback was multiple. In all cases, data demonstrated that using extrinsic feedback reinforced motor control abilities in children with CP producing functional and cortical reorganization.

Improvements by using extrinsic feedback in VR systems are probably due to longer training rehabilitation sessions where patients with CP can pay more attention.

This review encourages the work of multidisciplinary teams to create valid and reliable motor VR systems. Extrinsic feedback in VR with CP is a complement to traditional rehabilitation with clear improvements in motor disorders.

References

1. Rosenbaum, P., Paneth, N., Leviton, A., et al.: A report: the definition and classification of cerebral palsy April 2006. J. Dev. Med. Child Neurol. Suppl. 109(suppl 109), 8–14 (2007)
2. Gatica-Rojas, V., Cartes-Velasquez, R., Guzmán-Muñoz, E., et al.: Effectiveness of a Nintendo Wii balance board exercise programme on standing balance of children with cerebral palsy: a randomised clinical trial protocol. J. Contemp. Clin. Trials Commun. 6, 17–21 (2017)
3. Weitzman, M.: Terapias de rehabilitación en niños con o en riesgo de parálisis cerebral. J. Rev. Ped. Electron. 2(1), 47–51 (2005)
4. Oskoui, M., Coutinho, F., Dykeman, J., et al.: An update on the prevalence of cerebral palsy: a systematic review and meta-analysis. J. Dev. Med. Child Neurol. 55(6), 509–519 (2013). https://doi.org/10.1111/dmcn.12080
5. Morris, C., Bartlett, D.: Gross motor function classification system: impact and utility. J. Dev. Med. Child Neurol. 46(1), 60–65 (2004)
6. Márquez-Vázquez, R.E., Martínez-Castilla, Y., Rolón-Lacarriere, Ó.G.: Impacto del Programa de Terapia de Realidad Virtual sobre las evaluaciones escolares en pacientes con mielomeningocele y parálisis cerebral infantil. J. Revista Mexicana de Neurociencia 12 (1), 16–26 (2011)
7. Tarr, M.J., Warren, W.H.: Virtual reality in behavioral neuroscience and beyond. J. Nat. Neurosci. 5, 1089 (2002). https://doi.org/10.1038/nn948
8. Keshner, E.A.: Virtual reality and physical rehabilitation: a new toy or a new research and rehabilitation tool? J. NeuroEng. Rehabil. 1(1), 8 (2004). https://doi.org/10.1186/1743-0003-1-8
9. Lehrer, N., Chen, Y., Duff, M., et al.: Exploring the bases for a mixed reality stroke rehabilitation system, part II: design of interactive feedback for upper limb rehabilitation. J. NeuroEng. Rehabil. 8(1), 54 (2011). https://doi.org/10.1186/1743-0003-8-54
10. Reid, D., Campbell, K.: The use of virtual reality with children with cerebral palsy: a pilot randomized trial. Ther. Recreat. J. 40(4), 255 (2006)
11. Kent, M.: Diccionario Oxford de medicina y ciencias del deporte
12. Levin, M.F., Sveistrup, H., Subramanian, S.K.: Feedback and virtual environments for motor learning and rehabilitation. J. Schedae 1, 19–36 (2010)
13. Albiol-Pérez, S., et al.: Virtual fine rehabilitation in patients with carpal tunnel syndrome using low-cost devices. In: Proceedings of the 4th Workshop on ICTs for Improving Patients Rehabilitation Research Techniques, pp. 61–64. ACM (2016). https://doi.org/10.1145/3051488.3051517
14. Lünenburger, L., Colombo, G., Riener, R.: Biofeedback for robotic gait rehabilitation. J. NeuroEng. Rehabil. 4(1), 1 (2007). https://doi.org/10.1186/1743-0003-4-1
15. Molina, A.G.: Aprendizaje motor. J. Revista de psicología general y aplicada Revista de la Federación Española de Asociaciones de Psicología 48(1), 35–46 (1995)
16. Robert, M.T., Levin, M.F., Guberek, R., et al.: The role of feedback on cognitive motor learning in children with Cerebral Palsy: a protocol: In: 2015 International Conference on Virtual Rehabilitation Proceedings (ICVR), pp. 141–142. IEEE (2015)
17. Keough, D., Hawco, C., Jones, J.A.: Auditory-motor adaptation to frequency-altered auditory feedback occurs when participants ignore feedback. J. BMC Neurosci. 14(1), 25 (2013)
18. Roosink, M., Robitaille, N., McFadyen, B.J., et al.: Real-time modulation of visual feedback on human full-body movements in a virtual mirror: development and proof-of-concept. J. NeuroEng. Rehabil. 12(1), 2 (2015). https://doi.org/10.1186/1743-0003-12-2
19. Van Vliet, P.M., Wulf, G.: Extrinsic feedback for motor learning after stroke: what is the evidence? J. Disabil. Rehabil. 28(13–14), 831–840 (2006)

20. Subramanian, S.K., Massie, C.L., Malcolm, M.P., et al.: Does provision of extrinsic feedback result in improved motor learning in the upper limb poststroke? A systematic review of the evidence. J. Neurorehabil. Neural Repair **24**(2), 113–124 (2010)

21. Kita, K., Otaka, Y., Takeda, K., et al.: A pilot study of sensory feedback by transcutaneous electrical nerve stimulation to improve manipulation deficit caused by severe sensory loss after stroke. J. NeuroEng. Rehabil. **10**(1), 55 (2013). https://doi.org/10.1186/1743-0003-10-55

22. Vallbo, A., Johansson, R.S.: Properties of cutaneous mechanoreceptors in the human hand related to touch sensation. J. Hum. Neurobiol. **3**(1), 3–14 (1984)

23. Thikey, H., Grealy, M., van Wijck, F., et al.: Augmented visual feedback of movement performance to enhance walking recovery after stroke: study protocol for a pilot randomised controlled trial. J. Trials **13**(1), 163 (2012). https://doi.org/10.1186/1745-6215-13-163

24. Darrah, J., Hickman, R., O'Donnell, M., et al.: AACPDM Methodology to Develop Systematic Reviews of Treatment Interventions (Revision 1.2). American Academy for Cerebral Palsy and Developmental Medicine, Milwaukee (2008)

25. World Health Organization: International Classification of Functioning, Disability and Health: ICF

26. Moher, D., Liberati, A., Tetzlaff, J., et al.: Preferred reporting items for systematic reviews and meta-analyses: the PRISMA statement. J. PLoS Med. **6**(7), e1000097 (2009)

27. Patritti, B.L., Sicari, M., Deming, L.C., et al.: The role of augmented feedback in pediatric robotic-assisted gait training: a case series. J. Technol. Disabil. **22**(4), 215–227 (2010)

28. Choi, K.-S., Lo, K.-H.: A hand rehabilitation system with force feedback for children with cerebral palsy: two case studies. J. Disabil. Rehabil. **33**(17–18), 1704–1714 (2011). https://doi.org/10.3109/09638288.2010.535091

29. Chen, Y., Garcia-Vergara, S., Howard, A.M.: Effect of feedback from a socially interactive humanoid robot on reaching kinematics in children with and without cerebral palsy: a pilot study. J. Dev. Neurorehabil. 1–7 (2017)

30. Lopez-Ortiz, C., Simkowski, J.M., Gomez, W., Stoykov, N.S., Spira, D.J.G.: Motor learning in children with cerebral palsy with feedback of principal component space of reduced dimension. In: Pons, J., Torricelli, D., Pajaro, M. (eds.) Converging Clinical and Engineering Research on Neurorehabilitation. Biosystems & Biorobotics, vol. 1, pp. 311–315. Springer, Heidelberg (2013). https://doi.org/10.1007/978-3-642-34546-3_49

31. Sloot, L.H., Harlaar, J., van der Krogt, M.M.: Self-paced versus fixed speed walking and the effect of virtual reality in children with cerebral palsy. J. Gait Posture **42**(4), 498–504 (2015)

32. Baram, Y., Lenger, R.: Gait improvement in patients with cerebral palsy by visual and auditory feedback. J. Neuromodul. **15**(1), 48–52 (2012). https://doi.org/10.1111/j.1525-1403.2011.00412.x

33. Pu, F., Ren, W., Fan, X., et al.: Real-time feedback of dynamic foot pressure index for gait training of toe-walking children with spastic diplegia. J. Disabil. Rehabil. **39**(19), 1921–1925 (2017)

34. Pu, F., Fan, X., Yang, Y., et al.: Feedback system based on plantar pressure for monitoring toe-walking strides in children with cerebral palsy. J. Am. J. Phys. Med. Rehabil. **93**(2), 122–129 (2014)

35. van Gelder, L., Booth, A.T., van de Port, I., et al.: Real-time feedback to improve gait in children with cerebral palsy. J. Gait Posture **52**, 76–82 (2017)

36. Wood, K.C., Lathan, C.E., Kaufman, K.R.: Feasibility of gestural feedback treatment for upper extremity movement in children with cerebral palsy. J. IEEE Trans. Neural Syst. Rehabil. Eng. **21**(2), 300–305 (2013)

37. Tatla, S.K., Sauve, K., Jarus, T., et al.: The effects of motivating interventions on rehabilitation outcomes in children and youth with acquired brain injuries: a systematic review. J. Brain Inj. **28**(8), 1022–1035 (2014)

Can Motor and Cognitive Rehabilitation Work Together? The Example of Spatial Disorientation Treatment After Stroke

Francesca Morganti[1]([✉]) [iD], Paola Sabattini[2], and Roberto Casale[2]

[1] Department of Human and Social Sciences, University of Bergamo,
Bergamo, Italy
francesca.morganti@unibg.it
[2] Habilita, Hospitals & Research, Zingonia di Ciserano, Bergamo, Italy

Abstract. Our work aims to evaluating whether the motor rehabilitation and treatment of cognitive symptoms could have a synergistic contribution to the recovery of the patient after stroke. For this purpose, a case of hemiparesis of the lower limbs due to chronic stroke was studied in rehabilitation treatment carried out by the Lokomat technology for walking. At the same time, cognitive recovery in topographical disorientation was treated with the use of virtual reality simulations specifically developed for the clinical intervention. After a four-week period (twelve one-hour sessions) the participant (a forty-eight years old male patient) showed an improved ability in cognitive tasks that requires orientation in not simulated and virtual reality environments and an improvement in walking valuable from physiotherapy standards. Data will be discussed within the embodied rehabilitation approach underlining how cognitive and motor rehabilitation have to mutually work for the recovery of spatial orientation after neurological injury.

Keywords: Embodied rehabilitation · Lokomat-based physical rehabilitation · Virtual reality-based cognitive rehabilitation · Stroke · Spatial disorientation

1 Embodied Rehabilitation After Stroke

1.1 Embodied Spatial Cognition

The environment that surrounds us is not only made up of objects, but of elements that are spatially related to each other. To move in space, it is necessary to know the location of the individual objects in relation to oneself, to know how they are located relative to each other and to be able to evaluate and predict the mutual positions of the moving elements. The ability to navigate is therefore a fundamental requirement for moving in the surrounding environment. However, it may occur that, as a result of brain damage, injury or degeneration, the individual loses this ability with important consequences in terms of autonomy in everyday life.

In particular, the topographical orientation, which is mainly addressed by this study, refers to the ability to move in an environment without getting lost. This skill is acquired on three levels: knowledge of Landmark; Route-type knowledge and Survey-type

H. M. Fardoun et al. (Eds.): REHAB 2016, CCIS 1002, pp. 14–30, 2019.
https://doi.org/10.1007/978-3-030-16785-1_2

knowledge. In the first place, for the individual the spatial knowledge base consists in acquiring different points of reference within the environment (landmark). Secondly, the agent acquires the ability to combine points of reference and learns the paths that link them together. At this level the subject is able to construct a mental representation of a path from a starting point to a point of arrival using the different reference points he has learned. Finally, she/he will be able to develop the survey knowledge (i.e. wide-ranging). Thus, an agent constructs a type of topographic representation of the environment containing all the associated spatial information (i.e. monuments and paths) in such a way that the she/he deduces from it the entire environment, and she/he is able to estimate the Euclidean distances and possibly thinks of shortcuts that facilitate her/him in orientation. Having reached this final level of knowledge, the constructed representation is similar to a sort of aerial view. The acquisition of these types of knowledge provides therefore to the individual the precise and elaborate idea of a cognitive map of the environment. These three levels of acquisition are linked to a reference system that can be egocentric (referred to the subject) - for example "I take the road closer to me on my right" - or allocentric (requires the ability to imagine a point of view different from your own) - for example "I take the road closest to the bridge". The egocentric vision corresponds to the first two levels of knowledge (i.e. Landmarks and Routes), while the exocentric view at the third level of knowledge (Survey) [1].

According to this organization of spatial knowledge, an individual is able to interact correctly with the surrounding environment thanks to the spatial abilities she/he has. She/he is therefore able to perceive, act and operate in the world based on spatial coordinates. He is also able to determine spatial relationships with respect to the orientation of her/his body, to visualize the environment by capturing the movement and dynamism of objects, and to distinguish forms or to represent transformations, translations, enlargements and folds, or still, she/he is capable of mental rotation, understood as the ability to imagine the rotational movement of two-dimensional and three-dimensional objects. Space is therefore the dimension that embraces all things, but it is the agent that actively defines spatial relations and gives a precise position to all the objects of which she/he has experience [2]. An individual, in fact, is able to receive and acquire the necessary information to interact in the surrounding space by using her/his own senses: she/he will use not only the visual channel but also the tactile, enteroceptive, proprioceptive, and vestibular ones.

If spatial maps are organized in terms of paths that visually indicate significant points of space connected to each other (i.e. landmarks), this kind of organization is based on a self-centered space, as it is necessary that the agent has a knowledge of the environment strictly dependent on her/his own point of view. Maps are not, therefore, only representations that can support mental reconstructions of paths and sequences of salient points of space, but during an exploration the individual has the possibility to know that a previously done path exists within a set of possible spatial relations, each of which contemplates different paths better or worse than others. By this way, in fact, it will be possible to infer relationships between various points of the environment through reasoning processes in which the points of space can be recognized as neighbors even without having been explored directly (as, for example, the rooms of a building distributed over several plans). The environmental knowledge in this case allows you to have multiple perspectives that allow the explorer to have high-level flexible representations, able to allow planning-in-advance of the paths, joining points of the space never experienced as contiguous. In this way the explorers will be able to create abstract representations and to possibly put them in relation to each other in high-level organizations to be able to make inferences and plan routes in the environment [3].

At this point it is clear how each individual is able to develop spatial abilities as inherent in one's own corporeity from the first experiences with an external world. It happens however that, due to a congenital or an acquired brain damage, some individuals may appear as impaired their ability to perceive and act on the basis of spatial coordinates. As a consequence, they will not be able - completely or only partially - to grasp both the spatial relationships that exist between significant elements present in the environment, and those existing between their own bodies and the world around them.

1.2   Spatial Disorientation and Brain Injury

An important role within the multiple possibilities with which spatial skills can be shown to be compromised is represented by topographic disorientation. It presents itself as a clinical syndrome characterized by the inability to find the way in familiar environments and to learn new paths following focal damage [4]. The disorder can be a consequence of a progressive disease or derive from a brain accident such as stroke. Topographical disorientation following brain damage involves considerable difficulties in terms of autonomy and organization of daily life. For example, while using a map, the individual with spatial compromised skills can't cross the street in an unknown city, face the traffic, orientate her/himself in environments even if they were known to her/him. These are indeed all activities in the domain of space skills. Other examples may include reasoning skills, such as deciding whether a box is large enough to hold the objects she/he want to store inside, or the appropriate use of mirror images, such as putting on make-up while reflecting in a mirror.

Assuming that the primary visual abilities, the attentive capacities and the general cognitive functions are preserved, it is possible to affirm that the cases of topographic disorientation are typically described in terms of perceptive or mnestic difficulty. In the perceptive type (defined as topographical agnosia), the visual elaboration of places - including landmarks - and the exploration of space are altered, with the result of an internal representation of the environment very different from reality: patients fail to recognize specific characteristics of the landmarks, but recognize the categories to which the buildings themselves belong. In the mnestic type (called topographic amnesia), on the other hand, the visual and spatial characteristics of the environment are normally processed, but patients can't retrieve topographic information in order to orient themselves in space.

Aguirre and D'Esposito [5] proposed a taxonomy of cases of topographic disorientation distinguishing four categories of the syndrome. The *landmark agnosia* characterized by the inability to use points of reference for orientation. Patients are able to draw detailed maps and visualize places familiar to them before the onset of the disease; they can also distinguish between classes of buildings - such as houses or skyscrapers - but they are not able to identify specific buildings, such as their home or even famous places. Patients generally report that they are able to mentally retrace the route that connects one place to another, but an inability to recognize landmarks when exploring a daily environment. It is considered to be a consequence of damage to the part of the neural system specialized in the representation of landmarks, that is located in the ventral occipito-temporal cortex: fusiform gyrus (Brodmann area 37) and, sometimes, para-hippocampal gyri. Usually the lesion results as a consequence of a stroke affecting the right posterior cerebral artery. The *egocentric disorientation* describes the condition of those who are unable to represent the position of objects in relation to themselves even if they are able to identify points of environmental reference. Patients experience difficulties in recognizing or naming people or things but are able to accurately reach objects in space or to indicate the relationship between two objects (above, below, left, right, closer or farther). However, they can't do it in reference to themselves. Performance is also compromised in a wide range of visuo-spatial tasks, including those of mental rotation and wayfinding in familiar and non-family environments. The descriptions of the routes are poor and inaccurate and if they are asked to sketch the map of some routes, their productions are disordered. On the other hand, the recognition of visual objects is almost intact. This type of topographic disorientation is correlated with lesions of the right posterior parietal cortex. In the *heading disorientation*, people are not able to understand the direction to be taken from the points of reference they identify. Patients do not show signs of visuo-spatial agnosia and, in fact, they are able to determine their position using reference points. Therefore, they can't decide in which direction to proceed, starting from the points of reference they individuate, in order to reach their destination. Furthermore, the map drawing activities are compromised and they are not able to describe the paths between familiar places. The lesion, in this case, is borne by the retro-spinal cortex (posterior cingulate). The fourth category of topographic disorientation described by Aguirre and D'Esposito is the *anterograde disorientation* and includes individuals who have retained their ability to move from one space to another (wayfinding) in environments that had known at least six months before suffering the brain damage, but that they are not however able to orient themselves in new territories that fall within this time-span. The localization of brain damage in these individuals is similar (though without overlap) to that of patients with landmarks agnosia: lesions to the para-hippocampal gyrus. Some cases in the literature described bilateral hippocampus lesions and an extensive damage to adjacent structures in the medial area of the temporal lobe.

From this taxonomy it is possible to understand how the particular type of representation that an agent generates of her/his environment is dependent on individual skills, on the duration of the subjective experience with a particular environment, on the way in which the explorer was introduced into the environment (e.g. by passive/active exploration), on the level of differentiation of the environment and, finally, from the tasks that the subject is called to play within the space. Therefore, the multiplicity and heterogeneity of the strategies used makes it difficult to bring together in one single category the methodologies and interventions aimed at measuring and evaluating topographical disorientation. Thus, the interpretation of standard clinical test batteries is also articulated. It is, in fact, correct to underline how each clinical case requires an ad-hoc evaluation to design a rehabilitative intervention consistent to the identified clinical assessment. Generally, the behavior of the patient during hospital stay is observed in order to understand what is its degree of orientation even within the structure in which it is found, information is collected on the ability to perform family tracts and finally, of course, the spatial orientation neuropsychological tests are used.

1.3 New Tools for Spatial Rehabilitation

In recent years, the evolution of technology and the ever-increasing progress in research have allowed the use of virtual reality simulation systems for navigation and now they have become a widespread tool both for neuropsychological research, for assessment and rehabilitation [6].

A virtual environment (VE) is a three-dimensional computer-generated environment that users can explore and interact with in real time. Each virtual environment is composed of three elements: a content, a geometry and a dynamics. The content consists of the set of properties of objects in the environment. Each object is described as a set of properties and among the contents of a virtual environment are also possible a series of active objects - agents - to which it is possible to attribute interaction skills. The geometry of a virtual environment refers to the physical characteristics that the developer intends to give to the environment as a whole (e.g. two- or three-dimensional). The dynamics refers to the rules of interaction between the objects inside environment. In general, for a virtual environment to be credible, the objects contained within it must behave according to the normal laws of physics to which we are accustomed in the real world.

The success of virtual reality is not extinguished in the fields of entertainment or training, but has indeed found great applicability in the field of cognitive training and neuro-rehabilitation: virtual rehabilitation is a new therapeutic modality that offers the affected person feedback reinforced through a real and three-dimensional environment in which the user has the sensation of actually interacting in situations and with real objects. The computerization of the system allows the patient to receive relevant information on his performance and on the results obtained, to collect data and parameters of each exercise performed, thus providing the supervisor therapist with information on the progress of the treatment, in terms of accuracy, speed and effectiveness. In this way the therapist is able to create new exercises, calibrated and sewn expressly on the patient, respecting their characteristics and needs. The use of VR in rehabilitation has, in recent years, obtained more and more support especially because, compared to traditional methods, it seems an effective tool. Not only because, given its interactive and multimedia characteristics, virtual reality based exposure stimulates brain plasticity (i.e. the brain's ability to reorganize itself following significant experiences), but also because it has the advantage of being fun for the user who is interacting with tools created ad-hoc and perceived as more motivating and secure. Therefore, today, with the introduction of new rehabilitation protocols, if a conventional therapy is not foreseen for the brain injured patient, often a "virtual reality based" treatment or, if virtual rehabilitation is additional to the conventional one, a "virtual reality augmented" (augmented) is often mentioned.

On the other side, brain damage affects also motor abilities in patients and a motor rehabilitation is always requested together with a cognitive one. Recent evidence indicates that intensive motor training would be able to modify the neural organization and to effectively recover motor skills in brain-compromised patients. Every year there are many individuals who need it and take advantage of it: the loss of the freedom of movement that becomes poorly organized and disordered, the decrease in reaction times and the reduction of strength create deficits in the motor control that influence the person's ability to have an independent life and economic self-sufficiency. Recently, even in motor rehabilitation virtual reality offers the possibility of having, without renouncing methodological rigor, a simulation of everyday reality in which to stimulate the patient in the body movement. It allows users, in fact, to become main actors of what they are experiencing, just as they would be present in the movement acted in everyday reality. Moreover, the playful aspect, inherent in this type of technology, plays an important role for the involvement of people with brain damage, who feel more pleasantly involved compared to traditional activities standard rehabilitation has always used [7].

The most recent findings in neuroscience show us how the possibility of simulating an action, without actually accomplishing it, allows the passage from the concreteness of the action to the creation of cognition. Action, perception and simulation, as a whole, activate areas of the same functional networks, many of which are dedicated to spatial data (e.g. information on the location of an object, the direction of an action, etc.) and, since they also rely on the same functional clusters, it is possible to affirm that the understanding of the concepts is given by the basic sensor-motor simulation [8].

If we consider the dividing line between the perceptual, cognitive and motor system as more and more nuanced, it is possible to understand how, even in motor rehabilitation, being immersed in an experience, such as that virtual reality can provide, allows the patient to progress both motor and cognitive ways. The purpose of a rehabilitative intervention in an embodied conception (which does not separate motor activity from cognition) proposed here, becomes that of improving the ability to retain in memory the information on your body that interacts with the spaces and use them, activating motor processes related to the experience just passed to reproduce it in other contexts and ways. This is the idea developed by robotic rehabilitation within which Lokomat engine is based and constitute the main work hypothesis of the preset work.

The Lokomat robotic gait-orthosis (Hocoma AG, Volketswil, Switzerland) is by far the most widely adopted system to treat patients following stroke. It consists of a treadmill, a dynamic unloading system, and two lightweight robotic actuators that attach to the subject's legs. The kinematic trajectories of the Lokomat are fully programmable, and are adjusted to each individual's size and step preference. The complete device resides on a large parallelogram which is counterbalanced by a passive spring. The pretension in the spring is adjusted so that the weight of the Lokomat is compensated for, limiting upward or downward external forces to the subject during training [9].

According to the embodied view proposed before, a purposeful locomotion requires the ability to adapt individual goals and environment's burdens, and commonly involves concurrent cognitive effort about how to create consistencies between ego-centric and allocentric spaces while walking. Therefore, a Lokomat-supported gait performance cannot be considered a series of rote repetitions with each step exactly like the last because the environment is considerably variable and have to be understood in terms of "opportunities for action" - affordances. Instead, the work hypothesis we would like to introduce here is on gait as a complex task that places demands on motor and cognitive systems.

2 The Lokomat Walk Rehabilitation Supported by Virtual Reality

Nowadays the Lokomat, that is the commercial name for the DGO (Driven Gait Orthosis), is indicated as one of the best robotic device for use in individuals with chronic neurological disorders, including post-stroke hemiplegia. It consists of a powered gait orthosis with integrated computer-controlled linear actuators that assists and guides the hip and knee movements in the sagittal plane, while the ankle joint is not actuated. Lokomat has an electro-mechanical device, the BWSS (BodyWeight Support System), that guide hemiplegic patients while are walking on a treadmill. It is, in fact, generally used for gait rehabilitation and in lower limb movement disorders, especially in the acute and sub-acute disease phases.

It is considered as a stationary system that consist of a fixed structure and a mobile ground platform (i.e. treadmill). The treadmill gait approach uses a robot device connected to the patient's lower limbs together with the BWSS system, fundamental to off-load a part of the weight of the patient. The treadmill gait approach, in fact, consists of a set of cuffs connected to the patient's lower limbs, in order to support she/he to act the specific gait motor sequence ensuring a precise match between the speed of the gait and the treadmill. In the meanwhile, Lokomat is able to monitor gait motor parameters due to numerous sensors implemented, that not only assess the patient's performance but also ensure safety during the training exercises. Indeed, the limb exoskeleton is a wearable device that operate mechanically and simultaneously on the human body it can be considered as assistive devices for human impaired movement with a large range of degree of freedom (DoF), ranges of motion (RoM) and joint torque. It presents, in fact, sufficient DoF (a total of seven DoFs, three rotational DoFs at the hip, three at the ankle and one at the knee) as compared to the human limb to reproduce human natural motions and minimize the user's discomfort.

Moreover, Lokomat offers an augmented reality module that provide patients with the possibility to have interactive and direct feedback while walking. Generally this module is used to enhance the patient's motivation and give feedback during the exercise because the latter is mainly based on daily activities. Exercises, in fact, consists in collecting and/or avoid objects randomly distributed in a virtual environment. Among the most interesting Lokomat's characteristic there is the possibility to customize this kind of feedbacks by adjusting the movement intensity consistently with the virtual task difficulty. Thus, in each rehabilitation session the proposed exercises can be calibrated not only to patient's motor possibilities, but also to their cognitive needs, getting personalized.

According to Lokomat's characteristics our research question is: Can a motor impaired stroke patient improves in cognitive domains after a Lokomat-based walking rehabilitation program?

The present research aims in shed new light on how sensorimotor control processes, supported from a Lokomat-supported walk rehabilitation, and higher cognitive functions, such as the ones implied in spatial orientation, become more and more intertwined in complex movement tasks. The intent of the pilot study we presented is to understand whether and to what extent to use technology- supported motor training could also lead to spatial cognition recovery.

3 The Motor and Cognitive Rehabilitation Program

3.1 The Physiatrist Evaluation

The participant, that gave his consent to the participation at the study, was 48 years old at the time of the enrollment and has 10 years schooling age. He is male patient, about 98 kg weight and 174 cm tall. He suffered from a left hemiparesis due to stroke occurred in 12 years before his participation and stabilized after physiatrist rehabilitation. Specifically, his clinical description reports a severe left hemiparesis with hypotonic evolution in outcomes of stroke, dated 2006. At a neurological evaluation performed at the brain injury onset, the patient is alert, collaborating, oriented in the autobiographical parameters. He does not report swallow disorders, not verbal production disturbances. He had a left side hemiparesis with prevalent brachial expression. Specifically on the Right side: free right superior and inferior segmental movements, not limitations and/or stenosis. On the Left side: Upper limb with severe proximal-intermediate paresis with flaccid distal plegia, slight hypertonia at the reductive elbow (Ashworth 1); he presents active motility against gravity in shoulder abduction, a sign of recruitment at the elbow (F 1/5), not in the hand, pain in the mobilization of the left shoulder over 100° on the scapular plane. Finger flexion attitude, reducible, absent grips and pliers. Left inferior: hypotonic paresis (F 3/5 at the proximal level), not active dorsiflexion of the foot. At recruitment use toe-off orthosis, frontal plane position of the rearfoot (RSCP) in extension to the left. Good active control of the trunk, with the help of a single-stick stick rod for medium-short distances with a mowing left half-step.

3.2 The Neuropsychological Evaluation

In order to measure cognitive functioning, the patient underwent a standard neuropsychological assessment before and after the rehabilitation phases that included:

- Mini Mental State Examination (MMSE) for general cognitive level assessment
- Behavioral Inattention Test for excluding spatial neglect
- Money's Road Map Test for evaluating wayfinding ability
- Corsi's Test (Span and Supraspan) for spatial memory assessment
- Manikin's Test for up/down and right/left discrimination
- Benton Line Orientation Test for spatial pointing ability discrimination

Here a brief description of the test will be provided

Mini Mental State Examination (MMSE)
MMSE is a screening scale capable of highlighting the presence and severity of a person's cognitive impairment. It includes several tests that evaluate temporal and spatial orientation, short-term memory, attention and calculation, re-enactment, language (including naming, repetition, oral and written comprehension, reading and writing) and constructive apraxia. The maximum score obtainable is 30, beyond 26 the cognitive functioning of the individual is considered in the norm.

Behavioral Inattention Test (BIT)
The BIT is a battery of tests for the evaluation of visuo-spatial neglect. It is composed of 6 conventional paper and pencil subtests and 9 behavioral subtests. All the conventional subtests were administered: line barrage, letter cancellation, star deletion, copy of figures and geometric shapes, bisection of lines, representative drawing (a stylized man, a butterfly and a clock).

The Money Road Map Test (MRMT)
The MRMT is an evaluation made using a schematic map of a fictitious city designed to determine spatial discrimination. Some of the answers require an egocentric mental rotation in space. The stimulus consists of a dotted path that the subject is asked to follow, making sure to discriminate correctly between right and left. The subject is not allowed to rotate the map or make movements to give the correct answer.

The Corsi's Test (Span and Supraspan)
It is a measurement test of the "span" of visuo-spatial memory, that is the quantity of visuo-spatial information that can be retained in the short-term memory. The stimulus consists of a wooden board of 32 × 25 cm in which 9 cubes of 45 mm on each side are glued, arranged asymmetrically. The cubes are numbered from the side facing the examiner, not from the side facing the subject. In the span procedure the evaluator is seated in front of the subject and touches with index-finger the cubes in a standard sequence of increasing length (from two to ten cubes), to the rhythm of a cube every 2 s, returning each time with the index on the table at the end of each touch. As soon as the demonstration of the sequence is finished, the examiner asks the subject to reproduce it by touching the cubes in the same order. The number of cubes relative to the longest series, for which at least two sequences have been correctly reproduced, constitutes the score of the test which represents the spatial memory span.

In the supraspan procedure the aim is to evaluate spatial learning. The examiner presents a pre-set series of 8 cubes at the rate of a cube every 2 s. After each demonstration the examiner asks the subject to reproduce it and marks the sequence of cubes touched by the subject. The sequence is resubmitted until the learning criterion is reached (three consecutive repetitions) or up to a maximum of 18 tests.

The Manikin's Test
Manikin's Test is a test designed to assess capacity orientation. The test consists of 32 stimuli: on a white sheet a mannequin is depicted and, with open arms, holds two discs in both hands, one in black and one in white. The task requested is to indicate, for each

manikin, with what hand is holding the black disc, whether with the right or the left, paying close attention to the position of the manikin which is sometimes frontal (recognizable by the facial features and by the presence of buttons on the shirt), sometimes it is from the shoulders (absence of any stretch), others are turned upside down but frontal, while others are turned upside down in the back side.

The Benton Line Orientation Test

It is a proof of line orientation discrimination. Of the two parallel forms (form H and form V) the second was used for this study. Thirty boards are shown to the subject on which they are drawn two lines with different inclination. The subject must compare the inclinations of the lines present on each table, with a model on which are represented all the possible inclinations, arranged in a radial pattern. The score is given by the total number of correct answers and goes from a minimum of 0 to a maximum of 30 points. Scores below 26 are considered below average performance.

3.3 The Lokomat Based Motor Rehabilitation

The motor rehabilitation treatment was run for twelve one-hour sessions in a four weeks period by using the robotic assisted walking with Lokomat at Casa di Cura Habilita in Zingonia (Bergamo, Italy). Under the supervision of the physiatrist the patient was first allowed to walk in the Lokomat for up to 5 min in order to acclimate to the device and for the therapist to make minor adjustments. After this acclimation period, the Lokomat walking speed was introduced in a total of 12 trials.

For treatment with the robotic system, the amount of body weight support was initially set at 70% of patient's weight, then decreasing in accordance with load tolerance, although not providing <20% support. The selected speed was adapted to the patient's walking comfort under the supervision of a trained physiotherapist. Knee flexion during stance phase of walking was used as an indication for increasing weight support, and toe off during stance phase as an indication for reducing the weight support. Prior to testing, hip width, length of lower limbs of the exoskeleton, and size and position of leg cuffs were fitted to match the anatomy of the participant. Lokomat gait parameters (e.g. step length, patient coefficient, knee- and hip angles and their respective offsets) were set so that walking in the device was as natural and comfortable as possible. The patient doesn't have knowledge about how the robotic assisted gait training works. The accommodation of the patient to Lokomat lasted about 10 min.

The whole rehabilitative session was supervised by a trained physiotherapist, who instructed the patient at the beginning on walking modalities, and checked patient performance and cooperation, without giving any cue concerning motor performance to avoid extrinsic feedbacks. During treatment, Lokomat augmented reality module provide patient with spatial tasks. Patient was required to avoid obstacles or reach landmarks being forced to modulate walking accordingly. Several dynamic distracters were also present in the virtual environment to challenge subject's attention.

3.4 The Virtual Reality Tasks

The patient was exposed to four "ad hoc" virtual reality tasks designed specifically for the study. One important starting point for the realization of the tasks comes from the work of Claessen [10] and include an orientation task, a landmarks finding task, a wayfinding and a sketch-map. Here a brief description of them:

Orientation Task
The orientation task was carried out using the video Tour through Virtual Tübingen available on the Virtual Tubingen Project website (http://virtual.tuebingen.mpg.de/Project.html). In the movie, with a total duration of 50 s, a virtual tour of the German city is shown. The patient is offered a short path in which some turns appear at certain points. At the end of the video, the patient was shown four still images, coming directly from the video, which depicted the four relative turning points and was asked to indicate the direction he had seen in the video. A total of 4 points were awarded for this test, one for each still image presented. The score was then transformed into a percentage using a proportion. The video, which flows quickly enough, investigates the ability to know how to navigate in a city environment, choosing the right direction to take to reach a goal.

Landmark Recognition Task
The landmarks discovery task was made using a video, available at the following link https://www.youtube.com/watch?v=E8yxIfWbEGA, taken from a video game. Given the excessive duration of the film (39 min), it was shortened and cut in such a way that the patient was given the first 02.05 min and the fragment from the minute 04.18 to the minute 04.35. The subject was asked to observe the path that the means of locomotion would make, lending attention to the objects and details that he would have encountered along the way. At the end of the video, the patient was shown ten still images, coming directly from the video, of which five showed details that really they were present in the video, five instead showed some destructive elements (the fermi image had been "captured" in the video fragments that had not been shown at patient). The task for the subject was to indicate, responding with "Yes" or "No", if the detail shown in the image was actually present in the video. The maximum score obtainable is equal to 10, one point for each correct answer. The score was then turned into percentage using a proportion. The movie, which runs at a rather speed supported, investigates the ability to remember the points of reference encountered along a route executed for the first time.

Wayfinding Task
The wayfinding task was carried out as follows. The patient was accompanied by the operator along a path inside the hospital that was articulated along the three floors of the building. The route included 22 highlights, defined by the operator previously: for example, "turn right", "take the elevator", "pass the door". Thus, the patient took turns, took elevators and saw the number corresponding to the next floor in them. Once the path was finished, the patient was asked to replicate path backward, starting from the end to return to the beginning. The patient, always accompanied by the operator, indicated the way to go until returning to the exact point in which he had initially

started. The maximum total score is 22, obtainable if the patient remembers and correctly executes turns in all decision points. The score was then transformed into a percentage using a proportion. The task aims in investigating the ability to come back in a path just completed by remembering the points of reference.

Sketch-Map Task

For the sketch-map task, the patient performed a path along the three floors of the hospital. Once he has finished, it was asked to draw a map that depicted the route traveled. Considered the difficulty in making an accurate map of the explored environment we administered to patient a simplified version of the building map that summarily reported the rooms and the elements characteristic of each floor. In total the patient received three sheets depicting each of the three floors and was asked to trace with a marker the route he had just traveled. The subject therefore had to decide from which sheet/floor to start, indicate the exact starting point and plotting the route, remembering to also point out critical points such as "getting on the elevator", "Going upstairs/downstairs at the x floor", etc. A maximum of 30 points score has been assigned, corresponding to each decision point (e.g. go straight, turn right, take the elevator, etc.). The score was then transformed into a percentage using a proportion. The ability investigated is the ability to remember a path just completed and replicate it on a map, in a paper-and-pencil task, in which spatial cognition have to be turned from three-to bi-dimensional point of references.

At the end of the entire procedure a seven point Likert auto-evaluation scale (Way finding Questionnaire - Rooij et al. [11]) was administered to the patient in order to assess his self- efficacy degree in spatial orientation during everyday situations.

The Italian translation, realized specifically for this study, assesses the cognitive abilities and the degree of anxiety regarding navigation and orientation in everyday situations. It includes five subscales (response scale: 1–7): Navigation (2 questions), Mental transformation (3 questions), Distance estimation (4 questions), Spatial anxiety (8 questions) and the Sense of direction (9 questions).

3.5   Procedure

After a baseline motor and cognitive assessment, the patient was evaluated neurologically in four distinct phases cadenced by the Lokomat sessions: in total twelve training sessions were performed, every four training sessions standard or had-hoc cognitive tests were performed.

In particular, during the first meeting the participant received information regarding the aims of the study, the assessment procedure and the need to repeat the tests one month after the end of his stay in the clinic. The informed consent was subsequently collected. Once this preliminary action has been completed, the participant has been subjected to physiatrist assessment followed by the first cognitive assessment performed using the standard test battery. Regarding the neuropsychological part, the meeting is lasted about two hours.

Following the neuropsychological evaluation, the patient began the Lokomat treatment that had a total duration of 12 one-hour sessions distributed in 4 weeks.

After the fourth and the eighth session, using - when necessary – a portable computer, the patient was evaluated with spatial cognition ad-hoc tasks.

When the twelfth motor rehabilitation session was completed and the patient was evaluated through the standard neuropsychological battery to be able to compare with the data initially collected.

One month later, a final follow-up evaluation including the standard battery and the wayfinding questionnaire, aimed at measuring the effects of the long-term treatment.

4 Results

In the first neuropsychological evaluation the Behavioral Inattention Test result can exclude neglect syndrome and the MMSE revealed a good general cognitive level in patients (corrected score 28.89). On the contrary, spatial cognition evaluation from Money's Road Map Test, Corsi's Blocks Tapping Test, Manikin's Test and Benton Line Orientation Test revealed an impairment in the components of spatial abilities assessed from these tests. These score appeared to be improved after Lokomat-based rehabilitation treatment. MMSE remains unvaried. Detailed scores for standard neuropsychological spatial tests before and after physical rehabilitation are depicted in Fig. 1.

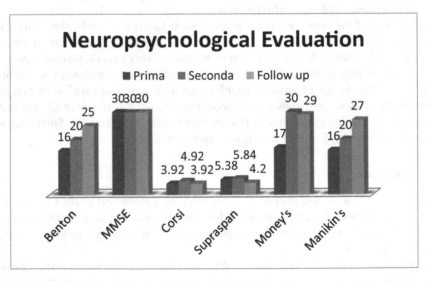

Fig. 1. Values (corrected for age and schooling age) in classical spatial orientation neuropsychological tests before and after Lokomat-based walking rehabilitation

Evaluation with the experimental procedure based on virtual reality simulations revealed an improvement in landmarks recognition, wayfinding and a sketch map task, while orienteering task appears to be slightly underperformed after Lokomat-based walking rehabilitation period. Detailed scores at the first and second evaluations are depicted in Fig. 2.

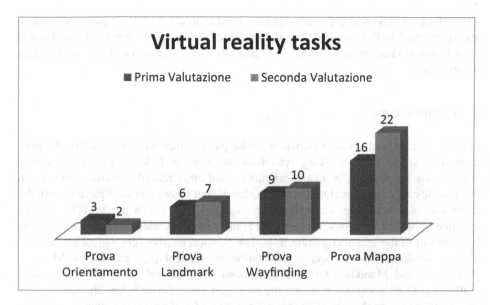

Fig. 2. Performances' score in the virtual reality based spatial tasks

At last, the patient appears to be slightly improved in walking tasks as showed from Lokomat Duration time, Length and Velocity parameters recorded in sessions 5, 9 and 12. Lokomat values are depicted in Fig. 3.

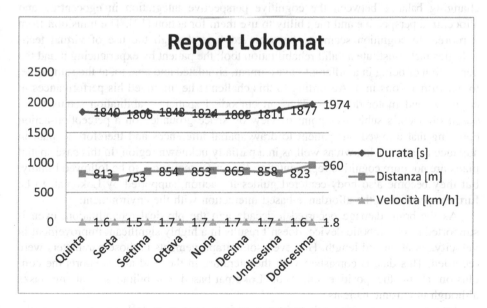

Fig. 3. Lokomat recorded physical parameters

Self-report wayfinding questionnaire revealed an average level of spatial orientation ability referred to the period before the brain damage. Impairments in spatial knowledge acquisition are referred to the last ten years as consequences of the neurological impairment.

5   Conclusions

Our data shows that a motor impaired stroke patient improved in cognitive domains after a Lokomat-based walking rehabilitation program linked with virtual reality stimulation. Specifically, in spatial orientation and other related cognitive tasks. From the neuropsychological evaluation, in fact, the patient shows a critical picture: with the exclusion of a not compromised general cognitive level (as in the MMSE) and the absence of neglect syndrome (as in the BIT) the patient revealed to have a score below the norm in all the spatial cognition tests. The classical neuropsychological assessment, in fact, originally showed spatial orientation impairment (e.g. as Benton, Money's Road Map and Manikin's tests), accompanied by evidence of impaired mnemonic skills (e.g. Corsi's supraspan below the average limits). Nevertheless the spatial abilities evaluated from those tests appear to be improved in the second evaluation ran after the motor training. Moreover, after four motor rehabilitation sessions the virtual reality based tasks (such as orienteering, wayfinding and sketch map) are carried out at average level while the landmark recognition appears to be poor. In session eight the patient revealed an improvement in sketch map tasks and a slight one in landmark recognition and wayfinding performance.

Topographical disorientation due to stroke have, thus, to be conceived as a changing balance between the cognitive perspective integration in egocentred and allocentred perspective and the ability to use them for action [12]. The transition from corporeal to cognition seems to be achieved here through the use of virtual technologies that constitute a valid rehabilitation tool: the patient by experiencing it had the perception of being in a different environment, simulated and able to, at the same time, to perform actions in it. According to this challenge he improved his performances in cognitive and motor domains. Thus an embodied spatial rehabilitation seems to be based on agent's subjective point of view on space grounded on a perception-action coupling that allowed our patient to draw spatial inferences and therefore to plan in advance a path in a known as well as in a partially unknown region. In this case spatial plans are not pure cognitive representation for action sequences to be followed blindly, but they become also body-centered guides for action, supported by Lokomat, to be further specified in the affordance-based interaction with the environment.

As the brain damage occurred a decade ago the physical rehabilitation, even if supported from a robotic device, doesn't results in a highly significant improvement in velocity, duration and length. However, some improvements in those parameters were recorded. This data is consistent with the literature in the field and supports the conclusion about the positive effect of Lokomat-based rehabilitation walking tasks although in chronic patients.

In conclusion, if it is true that virtual interfaces tend more and more to adapt to the "corporeity" of human beings, in this study human actions also seem to tend to conform to the interaction with technological artifacts. On the one hand it is not difficult to understand how technology can adapt to man, but the question remains to understand how the human mind can adapt, moreover so easily, to virtual contexts. Bateson [13] speaks of an ecological human mind, able to integrate with the surrounding environment through a continuous process of evolution. Thus, each technology has to involve in a different way human cognition which, interacting with it, acquire information relevant to the process of adaptation.

But how is it possible for an individual to experience new actions in a simulated environment such as the reality and, gradually recovering his skills, can really identify himself in a virtual version of himself to converge motor skills and cognitive? The answer can be in the embodied approach according to which action and knowledge acquisition are strictly clamped in a circular way. Accordingly, if an individual perceives the world in terms of spaces of possible actions, his motor impairment can influence also the creation of a cognitive map about the world in which he is acting with behavior limits. For the same reason to improve the possibility to move in an environment as with the Lokomat support can have influenced also his spatial cognition resources. In particular by observing the Lokomat parameters an increasing in speed, duration and walk length can be observed. These improvements seem to have influenced the patient ability in performing both classical neuropsychological and virtual cognitive tasks. Specifically, in the virtual reality spatial tasks, that provides to the patient a more ecologically like environment, a patient who is supported in increasing its walking speed and resistance (such as in length and duration) could have developed a more effective spatial attention that turns he in a more acute landmark perceiver. Moreover the increasing speed acquired with the Lokomat help could have facilitated the memorization of salient elements in space improving the orienteering and wayfinding abilities. Finally the enlarged length of the path achieved by the robotic support could have had a positive influence on sketch map task.

At last, this question will launch future developments of our research

References

1. Morganti, F.: Spatial cognition and virtual environments: how the interaction with 3D computer based environments could support the study of spatial abilities. Ricerche di Psicologia 26(4), 105–149 (2003)
2. Morganti, F.: Embodied space in natural and virtual environments: implications for cognitive neuroscience research. Commun. Comput. Inf. Sci. 604, 110–119 (2016)
3. Morganti, F., Carassa, A., Geminiani, G.: Planning optimal paths: a simple assessment of survey spatial knowledge in virtual environments. Comput. Hum. Behav. 23(4), 1982–1996 (2007)
4. Barrash, J.: A historical review of topographical disorientation and its neuroanatomical correlates. J. Clin. Exp. Neuropsychol. 20(6), 807–827 (1998)
5. Aguirre, G.K., D'Esposito, M.: Environmental knowledge is subserved by separable dorsal/ventral neural areas. J. Neurosci. 17, 2512–2518 (1997)
6. Morganti, F.: Virtual interaction in cognitive neuropsychology. Stud. Health Technol. Inform. 99, 55–70 (2004)

7. Gaggioli, A., Meneghini, A., Morganti, F., Alcaniz, M., Riva, G.: A strategy for computer-assisted mental practice in stroke rehabilitation. Neurorehabilitation Neural Repair **20**(4), 503–507 (2006)
8. Jeannerod, M.: Neural simulation of action: a unifying mechanism for motor cognition. NeuroImage **14**, S103–S109 (2001)
9. https://www.hocoma.com/solutions/lokomat/
10. Claessen, M., van der Ham, I., Visser-Meily, M.A.: Navigation strategy training using virtual reality in six chronic stroke patients: a novel and explorative approach to the rehabilitation of navigation impairment. Neuropsychol. Rehabil. **26**(5–6), 822–846 (2015)
11. Rooij, N.K., Claessen, M.H., Ham, I.V., Post, M.W., Visser-Meily, J.M.: The wayfinding questionnaire: a clinically useful self-report instrument to identify navigation complaints in stroke patients. Neuropsychol. Rehabil., 1–20 (2017)
12. Burgess, N.: Spatial memory: how egocentric and allocentric combine. Trends Cogn. Sci. **10**, 551–557 (2006)
13. Bateson, G.: Steps to an Ecology of Mind. Ballantine, New York (1972)

A Wavelet-Based Approach for Estimating the Joint Angles of the Fingers and Wrist Using Electromyography Signals

Rami Alazrai[1]($\boxtimes$), Mohammad I. Daoud[1], Ala Khalifeh[1], Nasim Alnuman[2], Yaser Mowafi[3], and Deena Alabed[4]

[1] School of Electrical Engineering and Information Technology, German Jordanian University, Amman 11180, Jordan
{rami.azrai,mohammad.aldaoud,ala.khalifeh}@gju.edu.jo
[2] School of Applied Medical Sciences, German Jordanian University, Amman 11180, Jordan
nasim.alnuman@gju.edu.jo
[3] School of Engineering and Applied Sciences, Western Kentucky University, Bowling Green, KY 42101, USA
yaser.mowafi@wku.edu
[4] School of Electrical and Computer Engineering, Purdue University, West Lafayette, IN 47907, USA
dalabed@purdue.edu

Abstract. The estimation of the joint angles of the fingers and the wrist using electromyography (EMG) signals is essential to enhance the quality of life for amputees, but this task is often considered challenging. In fact, developing robust mechanisms that can estimate the values of the joint angles in the hand provides better control of prosthetic hands and enables the execution of various daily life activities. In this chapter, we present an EMG-based approach for estimating the joint angles of the fingers and wrist. The proposed approach utilizes the discrete wavelet transform (DWT) to analyze the EMG signals in the time-frequency domain. Then, we extract a set of features based on the obtained detail and approximation coefficients of the DWT. The extracted features are used to train a set of support vector regression (SVR) models to estimate the joint angles of the fingers and wrist. To evaluate the performance of the proposed approach, we employed the publicly available NinaPro database, namely database 1, which comprises the EMG signals along with the hand kinematic data recorded for 27 healthy subjects while performing 52 hand movements. The results presented in this chapter demonstrate the capability of the proposed approach to estimate the joint angles of the fingers and wrist.

Keywords: Hand's joint angles estimation · Electromyography · Discrete wavelet transform · Support vector regression

© Springer Nature Switzerland AG 2019
H. M. Fardoun et al. (Eds.): REHAB 2016, CCIS 1002, pp. 31–45, 2019.
https://doi.org/10.1007/978-3-030-16785-1_3

1   Introduction

Nowadays, many individuals are living with missing limbs due to injuries caused by diseases, accidents, or wars [6]. Recently, the National Center for Health Statistics [1] has indicated that nearly 2 million individuals are living with missing limbs in the United States, with approximately 185,000 amputations occurring each year. Moreover, the number of amputated individuals is expected to reach 3.6 million by the year 2050. The ratio between the number of individuals who are suffering from upper limb amputations and the number of individuals who are suffering from lower limb amputations is one to four [1]. The percentage of the wrist and hand amputations is approximately 10% of the total number of upper limb amputations. In addition, 60% of the wrist and hand amputations are trans-radial amputations (i.e., below the elbow amputations). In fact, individuals who suffer from a partial or total loss in the upper extremities are facing several challenges during their daily life activities [5,6,8,19].

Recently, we have witnessed promising enhancements in the field of manufacturing wearable sensors and assistive devices. These enhancements have contributed toward the development of prosthetic hands that can recover significant functionality components of the lost hand. This, in turn, can improve the quality of life of individuals who suffer from amputations in their upper extremities. In fact, Merrill et al. [22] indicated that approximately 50% of the existing prostheses are controlled using the electromyogram (EMG) signals. The EMG signals are often used in prosthesis controls and rehabilitation support applications due to its ability to reflect the motor intention of a user before the occurrence of the actual movements [29]. Nonetheless, the EMG signals are non-stationary signals with time-varying frequency contents. This characteristic increases the difficulty of discriminating between different movements by analyzing the EMG signals and requires to employ a time-frequency signal analysis to characterize the movements of the fingers and wrist that are comprised in the EMG signals.

In this chapter, we provide a summary of previous studies that addressed the problem of estimating the joint angles of the fingers and wrist using the EMG signals. Moreover, we present our proposed approach for estimating the joint angles of the fingers and wrist based on analyzing the EMG signals using the discrete wavelet transform (DWT). The proposed approach utilizes the DWT to characterize the time-varying spectral variations of the EMG signals. Using the details and approximation coefficients of the DWT, we extract a set of features that characterize the joint angles of the fingers and wrist. The extracted features are used to build a set of support vector regression (SVR) models [15] to estimate the joint angles of the fingers and wrist. To evaluate the performance of the proposed approach, we have employed the publicly available NinaPro database, namely database 1 [13,14]. The experimental results reported in this study demonstrate the capability of the proposed approach in estimating the joint angles of the fingers and wrist for all the subjects in the NinaPro database. A preliminary version of this work has appeared in [8], which included a limited review of the previous work related to estimating the joint angles of the fingers and wrist using EMG signals and a brief description of the proposed approach.

The remainder of this chapter is structured as follows: Sect. 2 provides a summary of the previous studies that have been proposed to estimate the joint angles of the fingers and wrist using EMG signals. Section 3 describes the utilized NinaPro database, wavelet-based time-frequency analysis and feature extraction, and the construction of the SVR models. Section 4 presents and discusses the results obtained by our proposed approach. Finally, the conclusion and future directions are provided in Sect. 5.

2 Literature Review

Literature reveals that the vast majority of existing studies that investigated the recognition of the movements performed by the fingers and wrist based on analyzing the EMG signals are based on pattern classification approaches [4, 17, 23, 27, 30–32]. Despite the promising results obtained by these previous studies in classifying the EMG signals into different finger- and wrist-related movements, these methods suffer from the fact that it limits the myoelectric control devices to a predetermined and finite set of hand movements, such as hand opening and closing.

Recently, researchers have investigated control approaches that can achieve a natural and dexterous myoelectric control by applying regression methods to continuously estimate the joint angles of the fingers and wrist. For example, Hioki and Kawasaki [18] proposed an EMG-based approach for estimating the joint angles of the fingers using neural networks. The method presented in [18] has focused on a limited number of hand movements, such as fist with five fingers and grip with four fingers. In another study, El-Khoury et al. [16] proposed an SVR-based approach for estimating the displacement of the wrist while performing abduction, adduction, flexion, and extension movements using EMG signals. The proposed approach was tested on five healthy subjects and achieved a squared correlation coefficient (r^2) value of 63.6%. Similarly, Jiang et al. [20] utilized a multi-layer perceptron networks to estimate the joint angles of the wrist. The method by [20] focused on three types of wrist movements, namely the wrist flexion/extension, pronation/supination, and wrist radial/ulnar deviation. Ngeo et al. [24] proposed an EMG-to-muscle activation model that considers the electromechanical delay (EMD) between the onset of the EMG signal and the observation of exerted movement to estimate multiple finger kinematics using both fast feedforward artificial neural network (ANN) and a nonparametric Gaussian process (GP) regression methods. The experimental results reported in that study indicated that the GP regression model provides a higher estimation accuracy compared to the ANN model. In addition, Ameri et al. [12] proposed a support vector machine (SVM)-based approach to analyze the EMG signals associated with wrist flexion/extension, abduction/adduction and forearm pronation/supination movements. Krasoulis et al. [21] conducted a comparison between linear and kernel ridge regression methods in reconstructing finger movements. The results showed that the non-linear regression method outperforms the linear method. However, the performance of both methods was similar when estimating the joint angles of the fingers while performing movements that were not included in the training dataset. Alazrai et al. [6] proposed an ensemble-based regression approach for estimating the joint angles of the fingers and wrist based on the EMG signals. The approach presented in [6] extracts time-domain features from the EMG signals, and uses gradient boosted regression tree (GBRT) ensembles to estimate the kinematics of the fingers and wrist. The proposed approach was evaluated using the first iteration of the NinaPro database, namely database 1, and achieved an average r^2 value of 0.6.

One significant advantage behind using regression methods over classification methods is the ability of the former methods to generalize to novel movements that are not captured in the training dataset. Such a capability is highly significant for clinical applications, in which collecting training data that cover all the possible combinations of the fingers and wrist movements is prohibitively expensive in terms of time and effort. Having that said, this chapter presents an approach that utilizes wavelet-based features that are extracted from the EMG signals to train a set of SVR models to continuously estimate the joint angles of the fingers and wrist.

3 Materials and Methods

3.1 NinaPro Database

The NianPro database is a publicly available database that was recorded to facilitate studying the relationship between the EMG signals and hand kinematics in order to better control artificial limbs [13]. In this work, we utilize the first iteration of the NinaPro database, namely, database 1, which consists of the EMG signals and the hand kinematics data recorded for 27 healthy subjects while performing 52 different hand movements. The 52 movements are organized in three different exercises, namely exercise A, exercise B, and exercise C. Expertise A consists of 12 basic movements of the fingers, including the flexion and extension movements of each finger and the adduction and abduction movements of the thumb. Exercise B consists of eight isometric and isotonic hand configurations and nine basic movements of the wrist. Exercise C consists of 23 grasping and functional movements that mimic daily-life activities of the hand. During the experiments, each movement was repeated 10 times for each subject. The EMG signals were recorded using ten Ottobock MyoBock 13E200 active electrodes (https://www.ottobock.com), eight of these electrodes were positioned uniformly around the upper part of the forearm and two electrodes were placed on the active area of the flexor and extensor digitorum superficialis. The kinematics of the hand were recorded using a Cyberglove II dataglove (http://www. cyberglovesystems.com) that comprises 22-sensors, where each sensor provides a proportional measure of the angle between 22 pairs of hand joints. Figure 1 shows the locations of the sensors on the Cyberglove [13]. In this study, we denote the 22 sensors of the Cyberglove as θ_1 to θ_{22}. The recorded EMG signals and hand

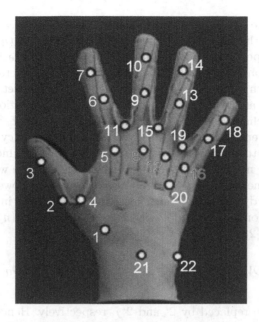

Fig. 1. The locations of the 22 sensors used in the Cyberglove II dataglove [13].

kinematics were synchronized at a sampling frequency of 100 Hz. Moreover, the EMG signals were amplified, bandpass-filtered, and Root-Mean-Squared (RMS) rectified.

3.2   Wavelet-Based Analysis of EMG Signals

EMG signals are nonstationary signals that have time-varying spectral characteristics. Traditional frequency-based signal analysis techniques, such as the Fourier transform, can quantify the frequency content of the stationary signals [2]. However, the Fourier transform cannot capture the time-frequency information encapsulated in the nonstationary signals [2]. Such a limitation makes the frequency-based techniques not suitable for analyzing the nonstationary signals [3, 7, 9, 10, 28].

The wavelet-based signal analysis is considered a remedy for the aforementioned limitation associated with the traditional frequency-based signal analysis techniques. Specifically, in the wavelet-based analysis, the wavelet transform (WT) is used to analyze the signals by employing a collection of wavelet functions [2, 26]. These wavelet functions are scaled and translated versions of a particular function, which is usually called the mother wavelet function. The mother wavelet function can be described as follows [26]:

$$\phi_{\alpha,\beta}(n) = \frac{1}{\sqrt{|\alpha|}}\phi(n - \beta/\alpha), \tag{1}$$

where α and β are the scale and translation parameters, $\phi(\cdot)$ is the wavelet function, and n is the time index. The wavelet function $\phi_{\alpha,\beta}(n)$ is translated in time to analyze a specific portion of the signal using the translation parameter, β. The selected portion of the signal is then expanded or contracted using the scale parameter, α, which is analogous to the frequency. The wavelet function $\phi_{\alpha,\beta}(n)$ becomes narrower as the value of α increases, and the location of the wavelet function $\phi_{\alpha,\beta}(n)$ changes in time according to the value of β. Therefore, the scaling parameter enables the capturing of the local frequency content and the translation parameter enables the localization of the wavelet function at a specific time index and its neighborhood. To implement the discrete wavelet transform (DWT), the parameters α and β are often selected to be powers of two, which are referred to as dyadic scale and translation parameters, in order to reduce the computation complexity [2,25]. The DWT of a signal $x(n)$, $DWT_x(i,j)$, is defined as follows [2]:

$$DWT_x(i,j) = \frac{1}{\sqrt{|2^i|}} \int_{-\infty}^{\infty} x(n)\phi(\frac{n-2^i j}{2^i}).\partial n \qquad (2)$$

where α and β are replaced by 2^i and $2^i j$, respectively. Hence, the DWT can provide an optimal resolution in both the time and frequency domains, which makes it more suitable for analyzing the nonstationary signals, such as the EMG signals. In addition, the DWT enables adequate description of an input signal

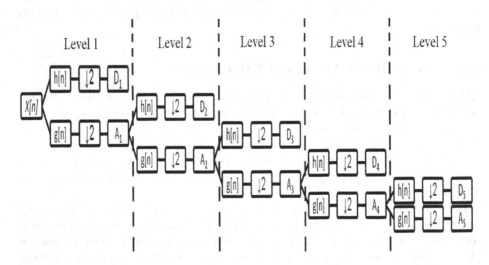

Fig. 2. Five levels of details and approximations DWT coefficients obtained for an EMG signals $x(n)$. For each level, k, the detail coefficients, D_k, are computed by filtering an input signal $x(n)$ using a high pass filter ($h[\cdot]$) that represents a discrete mother wavelet. The approximation coefficients, A_k are obtained by filtering the signal using a low pass filter ($g[\cdot]$). This process is performed recursively on the low pass approximation coefficients obtained at each level after down sampling the obtained filtered signal by two [11].

by generating a limited number of coefficients called the wavelets coefficients [2]. These coefficients measure the similarity between the signal and the wavelet functions.

In order to analyze the EMG signals using the DWT, we utilize a sliding window of size $M = 256$ ms and overlap size of $N = 100$ ms over each EMG channel. In particular, the Daubechies wavelet of order 8 was employed as a mother wavelet to decompose the EMG signal of each channel encapsulated at each window position into five levels of coarse detail and approximation DWT coefficients. Figure 2 illustrates the decomposition of an EMG signal, $x(n)$, into five levels of detail and approximation DWT coefficients.

3.3 Wavelet-Based Features

The obtained details and approximation coefficients at each decomposition level of the DWT represent different frequency bands of the EMG signals. In this study, we focus on five different detail-related frequency bands, including D_1, D_2, D_3, D_4, and D_5, and one approximation-related frequency band, namely A_5. In particular, we extract a set of features from the obtained detail and approximation DWT coefficients computed for each EMG channel. The extracted features at each window position per each EMG channel are:

1. The mean absolute value, which is denoted as MAV, is computed for each of the details and approximation coefficients of the DWT as follows:

$$MAV_{DWT_C} = \frac{1}{N} \sum_{s=1}^{N} |DWT_C(s)|, \qquad (3)$$

   where $DWT_C \in \{D_1, D_2, D_3, D_4, D_5, A_5\}$, $DWT_C(s)$ is the sth element in the coefficients DWT_C, and N is the length of DWT_C.

2. The standard deviation, which is denoted as SD, is computed for each of the details and approximation DWT coefficients as follows:

$$SD_{DWT_C} = \sqrt{\frac{1}{N} \sum_{s=1}^{N} (DWT_C(s) - MAV_{DWT_C})^2}. \qquad (4)$$

3. The coefficients of the fourth order autoregressive (AR) model are computed for each of the details and approximation DWT coefficients as follows [11]:

$$DWT_C(n) = \sum_{s=0}^{4} (q_s)(DWT_C(n-s)) + \xi_n, \qquad (5)$$

   where q_s are the AR coefficients and ξ_n is a noise term.

4. The entropy, which is denoted as ET, is computed for each of the details and approximation DWT coefficients as follows [11]:

$$ET_{DWT_C} = -\sum_{s=1}^{N} (DWT_C(j)^2) log(DWT_C(s)^2). \qquad (6)$$

5. The energy, which is denoted as EG, is computed for each of the details and approximation DWT coefficients as follows [11]:

$$EG_{DWT_C} = \sum_{s=1}^{N}(DWT_C(s)^2).$$ (7)

The dimensionality of the obtained features for each window position is equal to 450 features (45 features per each channel). This implies that the input dimensionality for our support vector regression model is a vector that belongs to $\mathbb{R}^{450}$, and the output dimensionality is defined to be the number of values measured by the Cyberglove, which is equal to 22.

3.4 Joint Angles Estimation

To estimate the joint angles of the fingers and wrist, we have developed a regression approach that utilizes the epsilon support vector regression (ε-SVR) model [15]. The proposed approach learns a vector of nonlinear mapping functions from the input to the output space, and can be described as follows:

$$\mathbf{Z}(n) = \mathbf{f}(\mathbf{F}_n)$$ (8)
$$= \begin{bmatrix} f_1(\mathbf{F}_n) \\ \cdot \\ \cdot \\ \cdot \\ f_{22}(\mathbf{F}_n) \end{bmatrix},$$

where $\mathbf{F}_n \in \mathbb{R}^{450}$ and $\mathbf{Z}(n) \in \mathbb{R}^{22}$ represent the extracted feature vector and the estimated values of the 22 sensors of the Cyberglove when the sliding window is centered at time n, respectively. The vector of functions, $\mathbf{f}(\cdot)$, consists of a set of unknown nonlinear functions that aim to estimate the values of the 22 sensors of the Cyberglove. For example, the function $f_1(\cdot)$ estimates the angle proportional value of the first sensor in the Cyberglove. In this study, the functions $f_i(\cdot), \forall i \in \{1, \cdots, 22\}$ are approximated using ε-SVR models. Specifically, for each function $f_i(\cdot)$, we construct a training set $\mathcal{D}_i = \{(\mathbf{F}_1, y_1), \cdots, (\mathbf{F}_k, y_k), \cdots, (\mathbf{F}_m, y_m)\}$, where $\mathbf{F}_k$ represents a feature vector, and y_k represents the measured value of the ith sensor of the Cyberglove. Then, an ε-SVR model is trained using the training set $\mathcal{D}_i$ such that for each $\mathbf{F}_k \in \mathcal{D}_i$ the ε-SVR model attempts to learn an approximation function, $\hat{f}_i(\cdot)$, of the function $f_i(\cdot)$ that has a deviation less than $\varepsilon > 0$ from the actual target value y_k. The obtained approximation function $\hat{f}_i(\cdot)$ can be written as follows:

$$\hat{f}_i(\mathbf{F}) = \mathbf{w}_i \cdot \kappa(\mathbf{F}) + b_i,$$ (9)

where $\mathbf{F} \in \mathbb{R}^{450}$ is a new feature vector, $\mathbf{w}_i \in \mathbb{R}^{450}$ is the ith learned weight vector, $b_i \in \mathbb{R}^1$ is the ith learned bias term, $i \in \{1, \cdots, 22\}$, and $\kappa(\cdot)$ is the Gaussian radial basis function (RBF) kernel with parameter $\sigma > 0$.

4 Experimental Results

4.1 Experiment Setup

For each subject, we have constructed 22 ε-SVR models to estimate the values of the 22 sensors of the Cyberglove. The parameters of each ε-SVR model are determined using a grid-based search that was performed along three directions. In the first direction we varied the value of the parameter ε, in the second direction we varied the value of the RBF kernel parameter σ, and in the third direction we varied the parameter $C > 0$ of the ε-SVR model that determines the tradeoff between the flatness of the approximated function and the amount up to which deviations larger than ε is tolerated. The parameters of the ε-SVR model that minimize the mean-squared error (MSE) between the predicted values of the Cyberglove data and the matching measured values are selected and employed to perform the evaluations described below.

In order to evaluate the performance of the constructed ε-SVR models, we have utilized a subject-specific five-fold cross validation procedure. In particular, each of the SVR models is trained using 80% of the data and tested on the remaining 20%. To quantify the quality of the constructed ε-SVR models, we have used the squared correlation coefficient (r^2) index. The r^2 index is computed for each function approximation $\hat{f}_i(\cdot)$ as follows [5,6,8]:

$$r^2 = \frac{(l \sum_{k=1}^l \hat{y}_k y_k - \sum_{k=1}^l \hat{y}_k \sum_{k=1}^l y_k)^2}{(l \sum_{k=1}^l \hat{y}_k^2 - (\sum_{k=1}^l \hat{y}_k)^2)(l \sum_{k=1}^l y_k^2 - (\sum_{k=1}^l y_k)^2)}, \quad (10)$$

where l is the number of testing samples and $\hat{y}_k = \hat{f}_i(\mathbf{F_k})$.

4.2 Results of Exercise A

Table 1 provides the r^2 values computed for the estimated 22 joint angles of each subject over the 12 movements of exercise A. In addition, Table 1 provides the average r^2 values for each joint angle computed over all subjects. The lowest average r^2 value was obtained for θ_6, which corresponds to the distal interphalangeal (DIP) joint of the index finger, and its value is equal to 0.54. Whereas the highest average r^2 was obtained for (θ_{15}), which corresponds to the metacarpophalangeal (MCP) joint of the middle finger, and its value is equal to 0.74. The overall average r^2 value computed over all angles and subjects for exercise A is 0.63.

Table 1. The r^2 values computed for the estimated 22 joint angles of each subject over the 12 movements of exercise A.

Subject	θ_1	θ_2	θ_3	θ_4	θ_5	θ_6	θ_7	θ_8	θ_9	θ_{10}	θ_{11}	θ_{12}	θ_{13}	θ_{14}	θ_{15}	θ_{16}	θ_{17}	θ_{18}	θ_{19}	θ_{20}	θ_{21}	θ_{22}
S_1	0.6	0.46	0.49	0.45	0.61	0.41	0.62	0.58	0.5	0.6	0.55	0.51	0.76	0.64	0.75	0.48	0.66	0.76	0.6	0.42	0.74	0.5
S_2	0.52	0.7	0.66	0.71	0.72	0.39	0.57	0.6	0.5	0.64	0.57	0.63	0.5	0.59	0.68	0.7	0.31	0.55	0.74	0.42	0.39	0.59
S_3	0.54	0.61	0.62	0.52	0.73	0.36	0.44	0.66	0.44	0.48	0.58	0.7	0.7	0.63	0.82	0.48	0.57	0.59	0.51	0.64	0.75	0.69
S_4	0.55	0.47	0.5	0.52	0.62	0.33	0.45	0.56	0.48	0.54	0.34	0.47	0.73	0.54	0.57	0.35	0.39	0.76	0.61	0.48	0.76	0.42
S_5	0.63	0.57	0.36	0.53	0.56	0.59	0.6	0.59	0.58	0.58	0.74	0.67	0.62	0.71	0.71	0.67	0.56	0.55	0.72	0.54		
S_6	0.69	0.65	0.57	0.7	0.67	0.62	0.73	0.7	0.73	0.53	0.67	0.8	0.88	0.86	0.74	0.56	0.66	0.79	0.82	0.69	0.89	0.74
S_7	0.47	0.53	0.38	0.61	0.66	0.48	0.37	0.63	0.71	0.75	0.67	0.79	0.74	0.66	0.76	0.7	0.63	0.76	0.7	0.55	0.78	0.68
S_8	0.79	0.74	0.76	0.57	0.46	0.44	0.51	0.6	0.39	0.67	0.52	0.52	0.58	0.57	0.75	0.48	0.73	0.75	0.77	0.56	0.54	0.71
S_9	0.68	0.54	0.42	0.64	0.39	0.34	0.47	0.49	0.49	0.52	0.51	0.46	0.52	0.57	0.51	0.55	0.42	0.58	0.65	0.35	0.59	0.8
S_{10}	0.73	0.63	0.47	0.49	0.55	0.73	0.7	0.65	0.58	0.75	0.6	0.59	0.66	0.66	0.88	0.49	0.57	0.41	0.7	0.47	0.73	0.47
S_{11}	0.72	0.71	0.79	0.73	0.67	0.63	0.65	0.77	0.78	0.71	0.65	0.41	0.8	0.64	0.77	0.75	0.59	0.74	0.86	0.64	0.79	0.84
S_{12}	0.34	0.57	0.6	0.35	0.43	0.33	0.34	0.67	0.37	0.6	0.51	0.73	0.72	0.59	0.73	0.66	0.58	0.68	0.6	0.41	0.67	0.52
S_{13}	0.42	0.63	0.51	0.58	0.69	0.63	0.67	0.62	0.6	0.76	0.63	0.71	0.8	0.7	0.77	0.61	0.43	0.67	0.73	0.61	0.79	0.66
S_{14}	0.45	0.34	0.34	0.42	0.5	0.69	0.69	0.54	0.49	0.59	0.56	0.5	0.6	0.62	0.68	0.45	0.59	0.25	0.53	0.6	0.62	0.32
S_{15}	0.53	0.61	0.51	0.57	0.56	0.52	0.7	0.67	0.62	0.83	0.57	0.77	0.81	0.77	0.78	0.74	0.68	0.69	0.77	0.66	0.83	0.61
S_{16}	0.82	0.71	0.66	0.63	0.74	0.56	0.61	0.74	0.55	0.57	0.64	0.68	0.37	0.42	0.78	0.68	0.4	0.71	0.69	0.62	0.35	0.74
S_{17}	0.77	0.61	0.71	0.47	0.7	0.45	0.74	0.69	0.55	0.63	0.63	0.68	0.87	0.8	0.83	0.58	0.64	0.6	0.86	0.69	0.86	0.58
S_{18}	0.48	0.4	0.56	0.42	0.61	0.48	0.63	0.64	0.48	0.49	0.58	0.68	0.8	0.7	0.85	0.54	0.58	0.65	0.68	0.49	0.83	0.54
S_{19}	0.48	0.59	0.52	0.34	0.52	0.45	0.3	0.66	0.58	0.54	0.52	0.65	0.73	0.85	0.66	0.58	0.63	0.53	0.75	0.45	0.45	0.48
S_{20}	0.63	0.72	0.79	0.56	0.74	0.72	0.69	0.76	0.71	0.84	0.7	0.83	0.81	0.81	0.84	0.68	0.75	0.67	0.83	0.68	0.7	0.65
S_{21}	0.52	0.77	0.67	0.47	0.68	0.44	0.61	0.87	0.62	0.79	0.54	0.6	0.89	0.68	0.89	0.73	0.58	0.56	0.85	0.67	0.78	0.55
S_{22}	0.38	0.57	0.62	0.75	0.71	0.55	0.44	0.6	0.57	0.74	0.57	0.58	0.74	0.76	0.54	0.61	0.64	0.67	0.66	0.54	0.67	0.82
S_{23}	0.85	0.71	0.66	0.62	0.7	0.61	0.46	0.76	0.63	0.71	0.74	0.79	0.9	0.83	0.89	0.8	0.81	0.7	0.84	0.71	0.81	0.65
S_{24}	0.68	0.67	0.77	0.63	0.83	0.77	0.65	0.68	0.44	0.49	0.68	0.7	0.68	0.53	0.72	0.66	0.64	0.51	0.48	0.66	0.45	0.72
S_{25}	0.58	0.61	0.6	0.59	0.85	0.77	0.71	0.81	0.58	0.65	0.77	0.81	0.79	0.72	0.8	0.61	0.67	0.79	0.78	0.62	0.82	0.65
S_{26}	0.57	0.65	0.6	0.48	0.65	0.71	0.65	0.81	0.51	0.65	0.64	0.78	0.79	0.81	0.88	0.73	0.72	0.76	0.73	0.55	0.61	0.79
S_{27}	0.49	0.52	0.49	0.6	0.56	0.59	0.6	0.57	0.56	0.61	0.54	0.64	0.73	0.54	0.56	0.55	0.59	0.66	0.56	0.56	0.38	0.66
Average	0.59	0.60	0.58	0.55	0.63	0.54	0.58	0.66	0.56	0.64	0.59	0.65	0.73	0.67	0.74	0.61	0.60	0.65	0.70	0.57	0.68	0.63

4.3 Results of Exercise B

Table 2 provides the r^2 values computed for the estimated 22 joint angles of each subject over the 17 movements of exercise B. In addition, Table 2 provides the average r^2 values for each joint angle computed over all subjects. The lowest average r^2 value was obtained for θ_{20} and its value is equal to 0.55. Whereas the highest average r^2 was obtained for (θ_{21}) and its value is equal to 0.74. The overall average r^2 value computed over all angles and subjects for exercise B is 0.70.

Table 2. The r^2 values computed for the estimated 22 joint angles of each subject over the 17 movements of exercise B.

Subject	θ_1	θ_2	θ_3	θ_4	θ_5	θ_6	θ_7	θ_8	θ_9	θ_{10}	θ_{11}	θ_{12}	θ_{13}	θ_{14}	θ_{15}	θ_{16}	θ_{17}	θ_{18}	θ_{19}	θ_{20}	θ_{21}	θ_{22}
S_1	0.76	0.52	0.66	0.66	0.68	0.70	0.75	0.73	0.68	0.68	0.82	0.73	0.78	0.76	0.85	0.77	0.68	0.74	0.56	0.68	0.79	0.76
S_2	0.84	0.79	0.76	0.70	0.75	0.77	0.75	0.79	0.76	0.67	0.81	0.72	0.78	0.65	0.67	0.65	0.79	0.75	0.75	0.62	0.77	0.87
S_3	0.71	0.47	0.59	0.67	0.78	0.77	0.67	0.80	0.79	0.69	0.61	0.81	0.72	0.53	0.75	0.74	0.67	0.65	0.68	0.54	0.71	0.77
S_4	0.65	0.37	0.54	0.51	0.68	0.70	0.63	0.71	0.74	0.56	0.73	0.74	0.74	0.51	0.68	0.70	0.72	0.58	0.48	0.37	0.71	0.62
S_5	0.67	0.50	0.45	0.65	0.60	0.64	0.69	0.59	0.63	0.73	0.69	0.67	0.68	0.72	0.88	0.70	0.63	0.70	0.73	0.57	0.63	0.79
S_6	0.79	0.60	0.66	0.71	0.77	0.74	0.70	0.79	0.70	0.65	0.88	0.80	0.81	0.80	0.86	0.83	0.75	0.84	0.72	0.71	0.84	0.47
S_7	0.76	0.64	0.59	0.61	0.74	0.77	0.68	0.74	0.76	0.68	0.82	0.72	0.82	0.63	0.81	0.77	0.77	0.70	0.63	0.54	0.85	0.70
S_8	0.70	0.66	0.67	0.70	0.69	0.60	0.69	0.67	0.61	0.65	0.71	0.66	0.68	0.64	0.71	0.60	0.62	0.55	0.66	0.48	0.70	0.79
S_9	0.65	0.62	0.60	0.59	0.71	0.65	0.47	0.68	0.71	0.47	0.76	0.66	0.77	0.48	0.71	0.61	0.69	0.54	0.62	0.37	0.78	0.79
S_{10}	0.68	0.48	0.58	0.70	0.68	0.63	0.40	0.73	0.68	0.65	0.65	0.69	0.75	0.53	0.81	0.69	0.65	0.60	0.42	0.46	0.75	0.66
S_{11}	0.81	0.54	0.67	0.79	0.75	0.83	0.58	0.75	0.86	0.58	0.84	0.69	0.81	0.61	0.72	0.67	0.73	0.61	0.49	0.51	0.83	0.82
S_{12}	0.66	0.62	0.57	0.64	0.74	0.77	0.71	0.81	0.80	0.73	0.80	0.83	0.82	0.71	0.82	0.80	0.83	0.75	0.65	0.55	0.86	0.65
S_{13}	0.62	0.52	0.43	0.71	0.69	0.63	0.61	0.66	0.69	0.69	0.75	0.61	0.70	0.66	0.71	0.63	0.67	0.68	0.50	0.52	0.69	0.86
S_{14}	0.59	0.48	0.75	0.56	0.67	0.63	0.58	0.65	0.66	0.55	0.75	0.66	0.69	0.64	0.54	0.61	0.67	0.69	0.59	0.46	0.71	0.75
S_{15}	0.59	0.60	0.48	0.54	0.81	0.68	0.49	0.86	0.73	0.81	0.65	0.81	0.66	0.64	0.59	0.78	0.70	0.57	0.50	0.53	0.72	0.65
S_{16}	0.78	0.69	0.68	0.74	0.73	0.59	0.67	0.74	0.67	0.69	0.88	0.78	0.78	0.77	0.71	0.76	0.68	0.77	0.54	0.75	0.81	0.76
S_{17}	0.86	0.71	0.83	0.50	0.85	0.81	0.73	0.88	0.83	0.74	0.78	0.79	0.84	0.71	0.74	0.82	0.87	0.76	0.76	0.60	0.85	0.78
S_{18}	0.64	0.49	0.44	0.52	0.73	0.70	0.56	0.76	0.73	0.62	0.74	0.72	0.77	0.59	0.75	0.75	0.73	0.64	0.53	0.45	0.64	0.83
S_{19}	0.73	0.60	0.68	0.73	0.80	0.76	0.76	0.77	0.81	0.77	0.78	0.77	0.76	0.69	0.75	0.82	0.73	0.73	0.72	0.57	0.91	0.90
S_{20}	0.68	0.64	0.74	0.82	0.84	0.72	0.79	0.80	0.72	0.90	0.78	0.71	0.75	0.57	0.79	0.73	0.70	0.82	0.69	0.69	0.89	0.84
S_{21}	0.84	0.83	0.74	0.78	0.77	0.75	0.76	0.81	0.75	0.91	0.85	0.77	0.80	0.81	0.74	0.78	0.76	0.79	0.63	0.57	0.88	0.93
S_{22}	0.74	0.55	0.69	0.66	0.81	0.80	0.56	0.77	0.82	0.74	0.73	0.77	0.78	0.50	0.56	0.78	0.74	0.55	0.68	0.50	0.81	0.77
S_{23}	0.69	0.65	0.60	0.62	0.83	0.75	0.71	0.78	0.74	0.69	0.74	0.82	0.77	0.61	0.77	0.77	0.72	0.59	0.73	0.32	0.75	0.58
S_{24}	0.74	0.73	0.67	0.65	0.87	0.84	0.73	0.87	0.84	0.73	0.86	0.86	0.80	0.78	0.81	0.87	0.80	0.75	0.75	0.60	0.88	0.72
S_{25}	0.76	0.62	0.68	0.74	0.77	0.75	0.64	0.69	0.74	0.69	0.85	0.74	0.77	0.68	0.81	0.69	0.76	0.69	0.71	0.62	0.75	0.77
S_{26}	0.82	0.77	0.67	0.86	0.83	0.75	0.87	0.86	0.77	0.85	0.89	0.83	0.79	0.75	0.87	0.79	0.80	0.85	0.81	0.80	0.84	0.76
S_{27}	0.71	0.55	0.42	0.66	0.70	0.66	0.70	0.69	0.68	0.69	0.76	0.65	0.75	0.68	0.75	0.68	0.75	0.69	0.46	0.59	0.69	0.66
Average	0.72	0.60	0.62	0.67	0.75	0.72	0.66	0.75	0.74	0.70	0.77	0.74	0.76	0.65	0.75	0.73	0.73	0.69	0.63	0.55	0.78	0.75

4.4   Results of Exercise C

Table 3 provides the r^2 values computed for the estimated 22 joint angles of each subject over the 23 movements of exercise C. In addition, Table 3 provides the average r^2 values for each joint angle computed over all subjects. The lowest average r^2 value was obtained for θ_7 and its value is equal to 0.45. Whereas the highest average r^2 was obtained for (θ_{11}) and its value is equal to 0.76. The overall average r^2 value computed over all angles and subjects for exercise C is 0.58.

Figure 3 provides two samples of the estimated values of the angles θ_{10} and θ_{11} for two subjects while performing two different movements in exercise C. In particular, Fig. 3a shows the estimated values of the DIP joint angle (θ_{10}) for the middle finger along with the actual Cyberglove measured values of θ_{10}. Figure 3b shows the estimated values of the MCP joint angle (θ_{11}) of the index finger along with the actual Cyberglove measured values of θ_{11}.

Table 3. The r^2 values computed for the estimated 22 joint angles of each subject over the 23 movements of exercise C.

Subject	θ_1	θ_2	θ_3	θ_4	θ_5	θ_6	θ_7	θ_8	θ_9	θ_{10}	θ_{11}	θ_{12}	θ_{13}	θ_{14}	θ_{15}	θ_{16}	θ_{17}	θ_{18}	θ_{19}	θ_{20}	θ_{21}	θ_{22}
S_1	0.50	0.40	0.57	0.60	0.70	0.57	0.68	0.63	0.66	0.85	0.85	0.71	0.72	0.58	0.80	0.58	0.58	0.58	0.82	0.47	0.71	0.81
S_2	0.63	0.69	0.47	0.60	0.57	0.65	0.31	0.60	0.52	0.50	0.84	0.63	0.61	0.51	0.70	0.67	0.60	0.47	0.58	0.51	0.60	0.83
S_3	0.49	0.55	0.49	0.45	0.61	0.54	0.36	0.56	0.52	0.52	0.77	0.60	0.66	0.49	0.74	0.51	0.43	0.55	0.78	0.45	0.65	0.53
S_4	0.37	0.38	0.47	0.51	0.31	0.34	0.25	0.45	0.31	0.44	0.67	0.52	0.64	0.54	0.56	0.53	0.45	0.51	0.62	0.35	0.64	0.69
S_5	0.56	0.48	0.44	0.61	0.55	0.47	0.49	0.61	0.39	0.65	0.77	0.66	0.54	0.60	0.80	0.66	0.45	0.50	0.78	0.47	0.62	0.55
S_6	0.52	0.60	0.64	0.50	0.67	0.61	0.50	0.79	0.51	0.65	0.77	0.78	0.61	0.57	0.81	0.77	0.55	0.54	0.82	0.59	0.66	0.87
S_7	0.72	0.58	0.52	0.64	0.67	0.70	0.62	0.69	0.65	0.49	0.72	0.70	0.70	0.46	0.75	0.70	0.69	0.60	0.72	0.53	0.59	0.80
S_8	0.46	0.68	0.50	0.46	0.62	0.45	0.34	0.60	0.29	0.18	0.62	0.59	0.28	0.15	0.60	0.52	0.23	0.19	0.70	0.45	0.46	0.64
S_9	0.44	0.40	0.34	0.50	0.61	0.60	0.44	0.64	0.37	0.44	0.61	0.63	0.55	0.37	0.64	0.58	0.52	0.40	0.69	0.41	0.67	0.68
S_{10}	0.35	0.39	0.54	0.48	0.63	0.46	0.54	0.56	0.41	0.37	0.74	0.63	0.74	0.23	0.68	0.62	0.53	0.39	0.65	0.57	0.72	0.72
S_{11}	0.54	0.62	0.58	0.54	0.71	0.56	0.45	0.78	0.52	0.56	0.86	0.75	0.63	0.48	0.80	0.78	0.52	0.41	0.73	0.60	0.69	0.83
S_{12}	0.58	0.48	0.52	0.71	0.66	0.68	0.63	0.75	0.61	0.60	0.85	0.74	0.77	0.62	0.75	0.65	0.67	0.66	0.76	0.53	0.70	0.83
S_{13}	0.40	0.51	0.49	0.53	0.69	0.50	0.28	0.68	0.28	0.32	0.73	0.69	0.49	0.34	0.69	0.64	0.39	0.42	0.74	0.44	0.50	0.59
S_{14}	0.51	0.45	0.55	0.42	0.63	0.44	0.29	0.66	0.42	0.41	0.66	0.58	0.37	0.31	0.76	0.54	0.39	0.33	0.79	0.56	0.39	0.57
S_{15}	0.49	0.45	0.60	0.50	0.64	0.40	0.62	0.64	0.49	0.41	0.69	0.67	0.54	0.50	0.68	0.53	0.38	0.45	0.76	0.48	0.61	0.78
S_{16}	0.55	0.54	0.67	0.56	0.63	0.53	0.34	0.62	0.49	0.29	0.78	0.68	0.49	0.28	0.64	0.60	0.47	0.41	0.71	0.35	0.52	0.71
S_{17}	0.53	0.59	0.53	0.56	0.61	0.57	0.48	0.60	0.56	0.63	0.78	0.61	0.54	0.59	0.66	0.69	0.51	0.51	0.76	0.54	0.64	0.71
S_{18}	0.57	0.33	0.45	0.59	0.58	0.49	0.36	0.66	0.37	0.46	0.73	0.71	0.54	0.50	0.56	0.66	0.53	0.57	0.77	0.46	0.54	0.80
S_{19}	0.42	0.64	0.43	0.50	0.51	0.55	0.46	0.70	0.51	0.47	0.70	0.69	0.46	0.36	0.60	0.63	0.43	0.41	0.59	0.49	0.75	0.60
S_{20}	0.54	0.56	0.51	0.60	0.64	0.45	0.54	0.62	0.43	0.50	0.76	0.66	0.38	0.57	0.71	0.68	0.43	0.64	0.71	0.50	0.74	0.73
S_{21}	0.60	0.82	0.72	0.76	0.78	0.70	0.66	0.77	0.59	0.63	0.91	0.82	0.67	0.43	0.78	0.80	0.72	0.73	0.85	0.57	0.78	0.75
S_{22}	0.35	0.65	0.46	0.40	0.69	0.42	0.41	0.72	0.48	0.39	0.75	0.74	0.56	0.30	0.71	0.71	0.55	0.43	0.76	0.51	0.72	0.62
S_{23}	0.41	0.57	0.42	0.48	0.62	0.48	0.47	0.54	0.51	0.52	0.81	0.68	0.58	0.52	0.63	0.62	0.54	0.53	0.73	0.55	0.56	0.82
S_{24}	0.68	0.62	0.63	0.78	0.71	0.51	0.53	0.73	0.56	0.70	0.86	0.74	0.56	0.65	0.75	0.75	0.62	0.49	0.86	0.65	0.67	0.78
S_{25}	0.54	0.63	0.57	0.56	0.69	0.59	0.47	0.69	0.54	0.48	0.77	0.74	0.59	0.53	0.68	0.71	0.57	0.58	0.76	0.49	0.53	0.71
S_{26}	0.71	0.61	0.66	0.54	0.64	0.44	0.34	0.68	0.55	0.34	0.85	0.71	0.55	0.32	0.73	0.63	0.48	0.51	0.79	0.46	0.79	0.89
S_{27}	0.62	0.49	0.51	0.56	0.66	0.68	0.33	0.69	0.54	0.59	0.77	0.62	0.61	0.50	0.75	0.61	0.55	0.54	0.78	0.41	0.65	0.63
Average	**0.52**	**0.54**	**0.53**	**0.55**	**0.63**	**0.53**	**0.45**	**0.65**	**0.48**	**0.50**	**0.76**	**0.68**	**0.57**	**0.46**	**0.70**	**0.64**	**0.51**	**0.49**	**0.74**	**0.50**	**0.63**	**0.72**

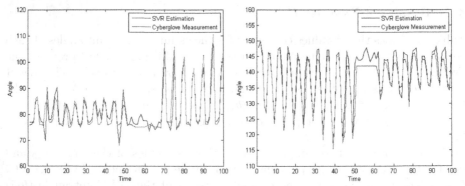

(a) The estimated values of the DIP joint angle (θ_{10}) of the middle finger for subject 1 (S_1).   (b) The estimated values of the MCP joint angle (θ_{11}) of the index finger for subject 21 (S_{21}).

Fig. 3. Samples of the estimated values of the angles θ_{10} and θ_{11} for two subjects while performing two different movements in exercise C along with the Cyberglove measured values of θ_{10} and θ_{11} [5].

5   Conclusion and Future Work

In this chapter, we presented an EMG-based approach for estimating the joint angles of the fingers and wrist using wavelet-based features. The performance of the proposed approach was evaluated using the first iteration of the publicly available NinaPro database. Experimental results showed that the proposed approach was able to achieve an average r^2 values of 0.63, 0.70, and 0.58 for the movements in exercise A, B, and C, respectively. Furthermore, the overall average regression accuracy measured using the r^2 index was 0.64.

Despite the promising results achieved using our proposed wavelet-based approach in estimating the joint angles of the fingers and wrist, there are several research directions that we are planning to investigate in the near future in order to enhance the accuracy, robustness, and applicability of our proposed approach. In particular, we are intending to investigate the following research directions. Firstly, we are interested in exploring the possibility of selecting a subset of the EMG channels to estimate the joint angles of the fingers and wrist, and study the effects of such a selection on the accuracy of the estimated joint angles. Secondly, we are interested in investigating the use of other time-frequency analysis methods, such as the time-frequency distributions [7,9,10], to analyze the EMG signals and extract kinematic-related information that can provide better estimation results of the joint angles. Thirdly, the results presented in the current work were obtained based on applying our proposed approach to the EMG signals that were acquired from healthy subjects. In the near future, we plan to evaluate our proposed approach using EMG signals that are acquired from amputated subjects. Fourthly, we are planning to investigate the use of deep learning approaches, such as convolutional neural network (CNN), to extract features from the EMG signals that can characterize the kinematic information of the fingers and wrist.

Acknowledgments. This research was supported by the Scientific Research Support Fund - Jordan (grant no. ENG/1/9/2015). Also, this research was partially supported by the Seed-Grant program at the German Jordanian University (grant no. SAMS 8/2014).

References

1. Centers for Disease Control and Prevention, National Center for Health Statistics
2. Adeli, H., Zhou, Z., Dadmehr, N.: Analysis of EEG records in an epileptic patient using wavelet transform. J. Neurosci. Methods **123**(1), 69–87 (2003)
3. Akin, M.: Comparison of wavelet transform and FFT methods in the analysis of EEG signals. J. Med. Syst. **26**(3), 241–247 (2002)
4. Al-Timemy, A., Bugmann, G., Escudero, J., Outram, N.: Classification of finger movements for the dexterous hand prosthesis control with surface electromyography. IEEE J. Biomed. Health Inform. **17**(3), 608–618 (2013)

5. Alazrai, R., Alabed, D., Alnuman, N., Khalifeh, A., Mowafi, Y.: sEMG-based approach for estimating wrist and fingers joint angles using discrete wavelet transform. In: IEEE EMBS Conference on Biomedical Engineering and Sciences (IECBES), pp. 596–599, December 2016
6. Alazrai, R., Khalifeh, A., Alnuman, N., Alabed, D., Mowafi, Y.: An ensemble-based regression approach for continuous estimation of wrist and fingers movements from surface electromyography. In: 38th Annual International Conference of the IEEE Engineering in Medicine and Biology Society (EMBC), pp. 319–322, August 2016
7. Alazrai, R., Aburub, S., Fallouh, F., Daoud, M.I.: EEG-based BCI system for classifying motor imagery tasks of the same hand using empirical mode decomposition. In: 10th IEEE International Conference on Electrical and Electronics Engineering (ELECO), pp. 615–619, December 2017
8. Alazrai, R., Alabed, D., Alnuman, N., Khalifeh, A., Mowafi, Y.: Continuous estimation of hand's joint angles from sEMG using wavelet-based features and SVR. In: Proceedings of the 4th Workshop on ICTs for Improving Patients Rehabilitation Research Techniques, REHAB 2016, pp. 65–68. ACM, New York (2016)
9. Alazrai, R., Alwanni, H., Baslan, Y., Alnuman, N., Daoud, M.I.: EEG-based brain-computer interface for decoding motor imagery tasks within the same hand using Choi-Williams time-frequency distribution. Sensors 17(9), 1937 (2017)
10. Alazrai, R., Homoud, R., Alwanni, H., Daoud, M.I.: EEG-based emotion recognition using quadratic time-frequency distribution. Sensors 18(8), 2739 (2018)
11. Alazrai, R., Momani, M., Khudair, H.A., Daoud, M.I.: EEG-based tonic cold pain recognition system using wavelet transform. Neural Comput. Appl., October 2017. https://doi.org/10.1007/s00521-017-3263-6
12. Ameri, A., Kamavuako, E., Scheme, E., Englehart, K., Parker, P.: Support vector regression for improved real-time, simultaneous myoelectric control. IEEE Trans. Neural Syst. Rehabil. Eng. 22(6), 1198–1209 (2014). https://doi.org/10.1109/TNSRE.2014.2323576
13. Atzori, M., et al.: Electromyography data for non-invasive naturally-controlled robotic hand prostheses. Sci. Data 1, 140053 (2014)
14. Atzori, M., et al.: Characterization of a benchmark database for myoelectric movement classification. IEEE Trans. Neural Syst. Rehabil. Eng. 23(1), 73–83 (2015)
15. Chang, C.C., Lin, C.J.: LIBSVM: a library for support vector machines. ACM Trans. Intell. Syst. Technol. 2(3), 1–27 (2011)
16. El-Khoury, S., et al.: EMG-based learning approach for estimating wrist motion. In: 37th Annual International Conference of the IEEE Engineering in Medicine and Biology Society (EMBC), pp. 6732–6735, August 2015
17. Gumus, C., Capa, E., Cotur, Y., Hasekioglu, T., Kaplanoglu, E., Ozkan, M.: EMG classification of index finger adaptive to prosthetic hand. Neural Netw. 1, 2
18. Hioki, M., Kawasaki, H.: Estimation of finger joint angles from sEMG using a recurrent neural network with time-delayed input vectors. In: IEEE Conference on Rehabilitation Robotics (ICORR), pp. 289–294, June 2009
19. Jang, C.H., et al.: A survey on activities of daily living and occupations of upper extremity amputees. Ann. Rehabil. Med. 35(6), 907–921 (2011)
20. Jiang, N., Vest-Nielsen, J.L., Muceli, S., Farina, D.: EMG-based simultaneous and proportional estimation of wrist/hand kinematics in uni-lateral trans-radial amputees. J. NeuroEng. Rehabil. 9(1), 1–11 (2012)
21. Krasoulis, A., Vijayakumar, S., Nazarpour, K.: Evaluation of regression methods for the continuous decoding of finger movement from surface EMG and accelerometry. In: 7th International IEEE/EMBS Conference on Neural Engineering (NER), pp. 631–634, April 2015. https://doi.org/10.1109/NER.2015.7146702

22. Merrill, D.R., Lockhart, J., Troyk, P.R., Weir, R.F., Hankin, D.L.: Development of an implantable myoelectric sensor for advanced prosthesis control. Artif. Organs **35**(3), 249–252 (2011)
23. Naik, G., Kumar, D., Arjunan, S.: Pattern classification of myo-electrical signal during different maximum voluntary contractions: a study using BSS techniques. Meas. Sci. Rev. **10**(1), 6 (2010)
24. Ngeo, J.G., Tamei, T., Shibata, T.: Continuous and simultaneous estimation of finger kinematics using inputs from an EMG-to-muscle activation model. J. NeuroEng. Rehabil. **11**(1), 1–14 (2014). https://doi.org/10.1186/1743-0003-11-122
25. Ocak, H.: Automatic detection of epileptic seizures in EEG using discrete wavelet transform and approximate entropy. Expert Syst. Appl. **36**(2), 2027–2036 (2009)
26. Rao, R., Bopardikar, A.: Wavelet Transforms: Introduction to Theory and Applications, vol. 1. Addison-Wesley, Boston (1998)
27. Sahin, U., Sahin, F.: Pattern recognition with surface EMG signal based wavelet transformation. In: IEEE International Conference on Systems, Man, and Cybernetics (SMC), pp. 295–300, October 2012. https://doi.org/10.1109/ICSMC.2012.6377717
28. Subha, D.P., Joseph, P.K., Acharya, R., Lim, C.M.: EEG signal analysis: a survey. J. Med. Syst. **34**(2), 195–212 (2010)
29. Tamei, T., Shibata, T.: Fast reinforcement learning for three-dimensional kinetic human-robot cooperation with an EMG-to-activation model. Adv. Robot. **25**(5), 563–580 (2011)
30. Tenore, F., Ramos, A., Fahmy, A., Acharya, S., Etienne-Cummings, R., Thakor, N.: Decoding of individuated finger movements using surface electromyography. IEEE Trans. Biomed. Eng. **56**(5), 1427–1434 (2009)
31. Yoshikawa, M., Taguchi, Y., Kawashima, N., Matsumoto, Y., Ogasawara, T.: Hand motion recognition using hybrid sensors consisting of EMG sensors and optical distance sensors. In: IEEE RO-MAN: The 21st IEEE International Symposium on Robot and Human Interactive Communication, pp. 144–149, September 2012. https://doi.org/10.1109/ROMAN.2012.6343745
32. Zhang, Q., Xiong, C., Zheng, C.: Intuitive motion classification from EMG for the 3-D arm motions coordinated by multiple DoFs. In: 7th International IEEE/EMBS Conference on Neural Engineering (NER), pp. 836–839, April 2015. https://doi.org/10.1109/NER.2015.7146753

Exploring Virtual Reality for Neural Rehabilitation and Phobia Treatment

D. Vargas-Herrera, L. A. Oropeza, O. E. Cabrera, I. Caldelas,
F. Brambila-Paz, and R. Montúfar-Chaveznava[✉]

Universidad Nacional Autónoma de México,
Av. Universidad 3000, 04510 Mexico City, Mexico
montufar@unam.mx

Abstract. The principal objective of neural rehabilitation therapies is helping affected people to recover their mobility and reduce their dependency to other people in personal and occupational life. The way neural rehabilitation therapies are applied used to be based on the experience of the therapists and the epidemiological data available. Meanwhile, computer games (serious games), specially, based on virtual reality, are already used to treat exclusively certain types of phobia considering that an effective therapy consists on exposing patients to the source of their pathological fear within a controlled and safe environment. At present, at National Autonomous University of Mexico we are developing a set of applications based on videogames technology, programming them by the Unity SDK. The idea is helping patients to recover their mobility, which was lost by a neurological accident, or to confront their phobia. In this work we present the corresponding advances. In the case of neural rehabilitation, we focus the applications for ocular, head and neck recovery, developing some 3D scenarios for the Oculus Rift device. Respect to phobia treatment we consider attending arachnophobia, acrophobia and aviophobia, developing some 3D scenarios for Card Boards and also the Oculus Rift.

Keywords: Virtual reality · Videogames technologies · Neurorehabilitation · Phobia treatment

1 Introduction

According the World Health Organization, in the world exists about one thousand million people presenting some type of disability, and most of them do not have access to medical attention and rehabilitation services according their disability, in particular in countries with low and medium income [1]. That means this group does not have the chance to get the necessary autonomy and health required for a dignified life.

Habilitation and rehabilitation are medical processes, which can help people with an illness to recover independency or become independent in all senses and consist of a group of activities such as medical attention; physical, psychological, occupational and language therapy and support. Moreover, in [2] we find The Convention on the Rights of Persons with Disabilities has established a compromise where countries must guarantee to people with disability the access to satisfactory medical services

© Springer Nature Switzerland AG 2019
H. M. Fardoun et al. (Eds.): REHAB 2016, CCIS 1002, pp. 46–57, 2019.
https://doi.org/10.1007/978-3-030-16785-1_4

(including sanitary attention, habilitation and rehabilitation services), without any kind of discrimination during attention [2].

In the other hand, we find that the Annual Health Report 2001 [3] of the World Health Organization was dedicated to Mental Health, the objective was to put in consideration the problems emerged from the mental health attention in the programs of global health and development agendas. Along with this enterprise, governments were invited to collaborate in the WHO 2000 initiative on Mental Health gathering information on the nature and extent of the problem, using the cross culturally validated Diagnostic Interview Schedule. In Mexico, the results of this effort were published in [4], where we find that the most commons mental disorders are specific phobia: 7.1% of population in Mexico presents one of these disorders.

At present, the use of interactive, 3D and video games technologies make possible to impact on the problems mentioned above, especially because it is possible to increase the number of patients that can receive attention at public specialized centers or at home. Also, the virtues of these technologies allow to check several human signals and activities avoiding the employ of a personal caregiver. Another virtue is that their use makes less difficult the doctor labor, helping them to monitor the therapy and control the patient activities. It means more patients can be attended by the same number of doctors.

The facts mentioned above where enough to begin to develop different interactive technologies in ours group. In this work we present some of the advances, in particular, the ones corresponding to the development of 3D scenarios for Virtual Reality systems. These scenarios were developed for motor rehabilitation of head, neck and eyes [5]; and also, for the treatment of different phobias: arachnophobia, acrophobia and aviophobia.

2 Academic Exploration

The development technologies applied to neurology since a scientific point of view are referred to 50 year ago. However, in this century is when the most important advances are presented. We find there is a high potential in the use of technologies for neurology due the possibility to improve human activities, these technologies were found applied in areas such as neural rehabilitation, diagnostic and neural monitoring, mental disorders, and other combinations of neurological and biomedical knowledge.

About five years ago we start to look for advances and projects corresponding to the development of interactive technologies and serious games applied to neuronal rehabilitation, and we find a few of these technologies, which were employed in hospitals by doctors and therapists as a reinforcement tool for conventional treatments and therapies [6–8], in particular they were using videogames. However, the user objective of most of these videogames were healthy people, in consequence they were not totally suitable for people with a disability. At present, we find projects sharing the same objectives and goals that to ours.

The next step after we laid the foundations for the development of videogames and virtual reality software for neural rehabilitation was exploring the use of these technologies in phobia treatment and we find in [9] some interesting works in the area.

At present, we can note the fast growing of interactive projects for rehabilitation and phobia treatment, this means we are introducing our workgroup in a promissory field of technological development with an encouraging benefit for patients with some grade of disability or mental disorder.

Finally, concerning the hardware, we decided to develop the virtual reality software (using the Unity SDK) for the Oculus Rift [10] (including the Leap Motion device in some cases), Google Cardboard [11] and recently for MetaVision [12] and Fove O [13].

3 Rehabilitation of Head, Neck and Eyes

A disability can be produced by a neural accident, leaving the person with cognitive and motor impairments, which affect its capability to live with total independency. The next action to take posterior to the accident is starting a therapy for an intensive rehabilitation, looking for the maximum recovery of the cognitive and motor functionalities.

After the neurological accident many patients will experience some type of visual disfunction. The visual effects associated with this accident can be categorized as sensory, motor and perceptual. In many cases, these disfunctions can be addressed by simple and effective therapies. However, in case of more severe accidents, patients are limited to move only their eyes or even not.

When patients are limited to eye movements, it is necessary to start a gradual motor rehabilitation therapy, where the first step is beginning with the ocular rehabilitation, followed by the head and neck motor recovery and then the arms, hands, and so on.

At present, the virtual reality technologies are employed in some therapies, but they are not considered as part integral part of them. The principal reason is that not always is possible to have the complete medical history of the patient, which is necessary to know if the use of the technology is acceptable for the patient.

In [14] is presented a study where is evaluated the employ of different user interfaces (2D, 3D, traditional and natural) with both stroke survivors and healthy participants. The results show that 3D interfaces exhibit better results in the motor domain versus a lower performance in the cognitive domain, suggesting the use of 2D natural user interfaces as a trade-off.

After considering these observations, as mentioned above, initially we decided to develop some 3D scenes for the Oculus Rift device to be used in rehabilitation therapies as an auxiliary tool always following the medical directions, instructions and considerations.

3.1 The Visual Field

The visual field is the observable space that is seen at any given moment, it is also defined as the restriction to what is visible. We note that when are performing eye movements the area of the visual field does not change, while when we are performing

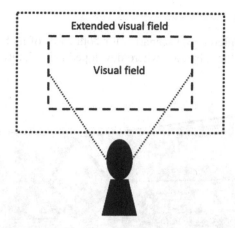

Fig. 1. The visual field.

the head or neck movements, the area is widen. In Fig. 1 we note the areas of the visual field for each case. In this work, we develop the dimension of the scenes according the type of therapy that will be performed by the patient.

3.2   Eyes, Head and Neck Training

The design of therapies for rehabilitation includes a group of movements or trajectory paths and the number of repetitions of each exercise according the patient necessities.

The scenes developed for eyes, head and neck training contain an attractive object, which is moving according the trajectory paths previously defined or programmed including a specific repetitions number. The trajectory paths are the arrange of different basic movements:

1. From ceil to floor vice versa.
2. From left to right and vice versa.
3. From the horizon to the proximity and vice versa.
4. From any upper corner to the opposite lower corner and vice versa.

During the trajectory of the object, it makes a pause at the middle of the path to have a softy tracking. By default, the patient carries out sets of ten repetitions for each trajectory. However, the number of repetitions and speed of displacement can be set via software.

When we are dealing with ocular rehabilitation, the trajectory paths that eyes follow are limited to the visual field due the head is fixed, meanwhile, when dealing with head or neck rehabilitation it is used the extended visual field because there are not limitations for the head movement.

The objective in ocular rehabilitation is the eyes of the patient follow the displacement of the object; no matter if the head is fixed. In the case of head or neck rehabilitation, the patient will also try to follow the object, which disappears of the field of view forcing to turn the head. Unconsciously, the patient must begin to recover their eyes, head or neck mobility gradually.

3.3 The 3D Scenes

We developed three different 3D scenarios for both cases of mobility recover training. As mentioned above, the scenarios where developed using Unity SDK for the Oculus Rift.

Fig. 2. Presentation of the menu to select scenario and type of training rehabilitation.

Fig. 3. Planet and Galaxy scenes. The planet is moving around the space according a previously determined path.

At first, when the user puts on the Oculus Rift, an initial scene appears exhibiting the menu where can select the scenario that will be used, and the type of training as illustrated in Fig. 2. In case the user is not able to select any option, another people can make the selection for him using the mouse. Once the type of training and scene are selected the user can begin the exercises.

Figure 3 shows the first scenario, which is a planet moving around the space. Before the planet starts to move around, a 3D arrow appears showing the direction of the next movement of the planet. The movements are performed according the trajectory paths defined by the therapist and were previously programmed. The user must follow with their eyes, head or neck the planet trajectory during some time or according the number of repetitions defined.

Figure 4 corresponds to the second scenario, which is a macaw flying in a jungle. Also, a 3D arrow is appearing in scene to show the direction of the flying of the macaw, this allows the user to know the training movements in advance.

Finally, Fig. 5 shows the third scenario, where a turtle is swimming under the sea, and the characteristics described above concerning movements are also exhibited.

Fig. 4. Macaw and Jungle scenes. The macaw flies around according a previously determined path.

Fig. 5. Turtle and Deep-Sea scenes.

4 Phobia Treatment Using Virtual Reality

Phobia treatment is an area where virtual reality has not been totally exploited. In particular, we have not found a virtual reality system with features such as engagement or motivation, designed and developed for phobia treatments. This fact motivates us to try to implement some simple prototypes that could be used by therapists to enhance the experience of the patients during their treatment.

In [15] is reported the strong preference by patients to use virtual reality instead of in-vivo exposure in phobia treatments. The inclusion of virtual reality in phobia treatments presents some benefits after being tested with patients who suffered from a particular phobia [16]. Moreover, the introduction of head-mounted displays such as Oculus Rift, Metavision or Fove-O, provokes an increase of interest in people to use virtual reality in phobia treatment schemes. Moreover, since these devices are sufficiently portable and economically accessible, there is a good chance for patients to undertake phobia treatments at home. In this work we are presenting three different virtual reality computer programs, one for each specific phobia treatment: arachnophobia, acrophobia and aviophobia.

4.1 Arachnophobia

Arachnophobia corresponds to a very strong fear to spiders, it affects between 3.5% and 6.1% of the population [17]. Meanwhile, claustrophobia and arachnophobia need therapy help to cure them because political action is not enough.

A pilot study was presented in [18] and reports the potential effectiveness of virtual reality in the treatment of arachnophobia. In this study is observed a significant difference on self-report cognitive and behavioral metrics of spider phobia between pre-test and post-test. On arachnophobia questionnaires, the scores of participants significantly decreased. On the behavioral avoidance test, participants were able to go significantly further through the different steps after treatment.

Considering virtual reality technologies are attractive, one could wonder whether touching a virtual spider could increase the effectiveness of the treatment. Especially since therapists usually encourage the patients to touch the spider during in vivo exposure and modeling exercises.

Figure 6 presents the scenarios we developed for Oculus Rift and Google Cardboard. The reason to develop 3D environments for a cardboard is because actually almost all students (and people) have a smartphone and they will be able to use them.

Fig. 6. Oculus Rift and Google cardboard environments for arachnophobia treatment.

54   D. Vargas-Herrera et al.

We can check that the environment for Oculus Rift has more details and resolution that the ones for cardboard.

4.2 Acrophobia

Acrophobia is defined as an irrational fear of heights, especially when one is not particularly high up. Acrophobia belongs to a category of specific phobias, presenting a space and motion discomfort. About 5% of the general population suffer from acrophobia [19].

The combined benefits (flexibility and confidentiality, possibility to create and control, etc.) of virtual reality approaches suggest that it holds great promise as a therapeutic tool for enhancing acrophobia treatment outcomes [19].

Figure 7 shows the environment we developed for Oculus Rift. The theme of the scenarios is an amusement park, where different situations concerning to heights are presented. The environment also includes auditive stimuli.

Fig. 7. Oculus Rift environments for agoraphobia treatment.

4.3   Aviophobia

Aviophobia is a fear of being on an airplane, or other flying vehicle, such as a helicopter, while in flight. It is also referred to as flying phobia, flight phobia or fear of flying.

It is a serious problem that affects millions of individuals. It has been estimated that 10–25% of the general population suffer this phobia [20].

The exposure therapy for aviophobia used to be an effective technique. However, this therapy is expensive, logistically difficult, and presents significant problems of patient confidentiality and potential embarrassment. The exposure therapy is usually provided in stages with patients first practicing going to an airport, seeing and hearing the sights and sounds of airplanes taking off and landing. Subsequently they might actually enter and sit in a stationary airplane. Ideally a flight experience would be the capstone of the therapy program.

The virtual reality exposure has been shown in a controlled study to be an effective treatment approach [20] because the patient is exposed to a virtual environment containing the feared stimulus. For that reason, we decided to develop an airport environment for a cardboard that could act as a tool for aviophobia treatment.

Figure 8 shows the environment we developed corresponding to Terminal 2 of Mexico City Airport. The idea is the user arrives to airport and moves around it until finds its seat on an airplane.

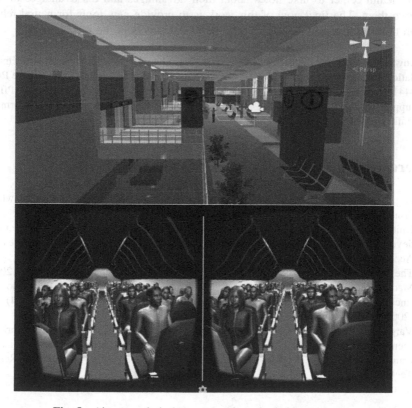

Fig. 8. Airport and airplane scenes for aviophobia treatment.

5   Conclusions and Further Work

We have presented some advances in virtual reality we have carried out in last five years. The environments we have developed are intended for neural rehabilitation and phobia treatments, both activities are concerned the neurology area.

We have used the Unity SDK as a standard platform in conjunction with Google cardboard, Oculus Rift and Leap Motion SDK. We are actually exploring Metavision and Fove-O for future works.

At this point we are more interested in academic use of these technologies than in clinical application. Virtual reality is very attractive and motivational to computer engineering students. The use of devices such as Oculus Rift, Leap Motion, Metavision, Fove-O and Google cardboard, and the development of scenes and programs on the Unity platform gives them another abilities, perspectives and opportunities for their professional life.

We pretend that the software developed for cardboard can be used for students of neurology, biology, psychology and biomedical engineering considering the extended use of smartphones and a cardboard is cheap or can be easily developed.

Finally, the use of virtual reality for some cases of neural rehabilitation and phobia treatment is innovative in Mexico. The expectation is to transfer our developments to a public health center to take notes about their advantages and disadvantages to could improve them. The final goal of this work is to provide new tools for neural rehabilitation that improve such task and offer new alternatives in the medical field.

Acknowledgments. We thanks to the Dirección General de Asuntos del Personal Académico of the National Autonomous University of Mexico, through PAPIME for the support of the Project PE104416 "Ambientes Virtuales y Herramientas Digitales para Neurociencias" and PAPIIT for the support of the Project IT101917 "Realidad Virtual en la Visualización de Información Geográfica y Geofísica."

References

1. Organización Mundial de la Salud. Discapacidades y Rehabilitación. http://www.who.int/disabilities/care/es/. Accessed 29 Sept 2018
2. United Nations: Convention on the rights of persons with disabilities. https://www.un.org/development/desa/disabilities/convention-on-the-rights-of-persons-with-disabilities.html. Accessed 29 Sept 2018
3. The World Health Report: 2001: Mental Health: New Understanding, New Hope (2001)
4. Medina, M., et al.: Prevalencia de trastornos mentales y uso de servicios: Resultados de la Encuesta Nacional de Epidemiología Psiquiátrica en México. Salud Mental **26**(4), 1–16 (2003)
5. Vargas-Herrera, D., Brambila-Paz, F., Caldelas, I., Montufar-Chaveznava, R.: Exploring 3D scenes for neurorehabilitation. In: Fardoun, H.M., Ruiz-Penichet, V., Alghazzawi, D.M., Gamito, P. (eds.) 4th Workshop on ICTs for improving Patients Rehabilitation Research Techniques (REHAB 2016), pp. 77–80. ACM, New York (2016)
6. VirtualRehab. https://evolvrehab.com/virtualrehab. Accessed 30 Sept 2018

7. Virtual Reality: Kinect Rehabilitation. http://www.virtual-reality-rehabilitation.com. Accessed 30 Sept 2018
8. Reflexion health. http://reflexionhealth.com. Accessed 30 Sept 2018
9. Wiederhold, B.K., Bouchard, S.: Advances in Virtual Reality and Anxiety Disorders. Series in Anxiety and Related Disorders, 1st edn. Springer, New York (2014). https://doi.org/10.1007/978-1-4899-8023-6
10. Oculus Rift. https://www.oculus.com/rift. Accessed 29 Sept 2018
11. Google Cardboard. https://vr.google.com/cardboard. Accessed 29 Sept 2019
12. Metavision. https://www.metavision.com. Accessed 29 Sept 2018
13. Fove O. https://www.getfove.com. Accessed 29 Sept 2018
14. Vourvopoulos, A., Faria, A.L., Cameirão, M., Bermúdez i Badia, S.: Quantifying cognitive-motor interference in virtual reality training after stroke: the role of interfaces. In: Sharkey, P.M., Pareto, L., Broeren, J., Rydmark, M. (eds.) 10th International Conference on Disability, Virtual Reality and Associated Technologies, pp. 45–53. The University of Reading, Gothenburg (2014)
15. Garcia-Palacios, A., Hoffman, H., Carlin, A., Furness, T.A., Botella, C.: Virtual reality in the treatment of spider phobia: a controlled study. Behav. Res. Ther. 40, 983–993 (2002)
16. Trigo-Algar, A.R.: Serious games for overcoming phobias: the benefits of game elements. Master's degree Project in Informatics. University of Skövde (2014)
17. Schmitt, W.J., Müri, R.M.: Neurobiologie der spinnenphobie. Schweizer Archiv für Neurologie 160(8), 352–355 (2009)
18. Bouchard, S., Côté, S., St-Jacques, J., Robillard, G., Renaud, P.: Effectiveness of virtual reality exposure in the treatment of arachnophobia using 3D games. Technol. Healthc. 14(1), 19–27 (2006)
19. Coelho, C., Waters, A., Hine, T., Wallis, G.: The use of virtual reality in acrophobia research and treatment. J. Anxiety Disord. 23(5), 563–574 (2009)
20. Hodges, L., Rothbaum, B., Watson, B., Kessler, G.D., Opdyke, D.: Virtual reality exposure for fear of flying therapy. IEEE Comput. Graphics Appl. 16(6), 42–49 (1999)

Interactive Systems Proposal for Psychomotor Rehabilitation in Hearing Impaired Children

Victor M. Peñeñory[1(✉)], Cristina Manresa-Yee[2],
Inmaculada Riquelme[3,4], Cesar A. Collazos[5], Habib M. Fardoun[6],
and Daniyal M. Alghazzawi[7]

[1] University of San Buenaventura, Ave. 10 de Mayo, La Umbria, Cali, Colombia
vmpeneno@usbcali.edu.co
[2] University of the Balearic Islands,
Crta. Valldemossa, km 7.5, 07122 Palma, Spain
cristina.manresa@uib.es
[3] Department of Nursing and Physiotherapy,
University of the Balearic Islands, Palma, Spain
inma.riquelme@uib.es
[4] University Institute of Health Sciences Research (IUNICS-Idisba),
University of Balearic Islands, Palma, Spain
[5] University of Cauca, Cll 5 no. 4-70, Popayan, Colombia
ccollazo@unicauca.edu.co
[6] Ahlia University, Bld 41 Rd 18 Al-Hoora 310, Manama, Bahrain
hfardoun@ahlia.edu.bh
[7] University of King Abdulaziz, Jeddah 21589, Kingdom of Saudi Arabia
dghazzawi@kau.edu.sa

Abstract. Research reports psychomotor deficits and delays in children with hearing impairment (HI) due to hearing deprivation and its consequences. In this paper, we examine the basic psychomotor deficits of individuals with HI and review the literature to compile systems that help train and improve their psychomotor skills, and then propose some interactive systems that can be used as tools for the psychomotor rehabilitation of children with HI.

Keywords: Psychomotor development · Psychomotor deficits ·
Hearing impairment · Children with special needs · Sensors ·
Interactive systems

1 Introduction

Psychomotricity integrates the cognitive, emotional, symbolical and physical interactions in the individual's capacity to be and to act in a psychosocial context [1]. During the child's development, the acquisition in motor performance sets the basis for posterior complex psychological abilities, such as the symbolism or the impulsivity

V. M. Peñeñory, C. Manresa-Yee, I. Riquelme, C. A. Collazos and H. M. Fardoun—These authors contributed equally to this work.

regulation. Therefore, the adequate development of basic psychomotor areas, such as body schema (related to body awareness) and body image (related to self-esteem), posture, balance, gross and fine motor skills, space and rhythm may determine the successful achievement of future cognitive, emotional or social processes.

Hearing impaired (HI) children can present hearing loss levels varying from mild to profound. The auditory deprivation and concomitant processes such as vestibular damage may interfere in the sensorimotor function, which produces an especial development of their psychomotor abilities. Research reports deficits and delays for HI children in their psychomotor development in motor skill performance, balance, dynamic coordination, visuomotor coordination, among others [2–5].

The aim of this paper is to (1) examine the basic psychomotor deficits of individuals with HI (Sect. 2), (2) review the literature to compile systems that help train and improve psychomotor skills in this population (Sect. 3), and (3) propose some ideas for interactive systems for psychomotor rehabilitation in children with HI (Sect. 4).

2 Psychomotor Deficits in Individuals with HI

Psychomotricity is defined as the individual's ability to act in a psychosocial context, by the integration of physical, emotional, cognitive and symbolical interactions [1]. An appropriate motor development during the childhood is a fundamental premise for the further acquisition of high-level psychological resources, such as symbolism or lability regulation. Thus, complex abilities for cognition, emotion and social interactions are determined by the development of basic psychomotor areas, such as body perception (fundamental for body awareness and self-steem), gross (i.e. posture, balance) and fine (manipulation) motor function, space, time and rhythm [1]. Psychomotor skills are usually classified into fundamental (i.e. body perception, posture, balance and coordination), perceptual (i.e. space, time and rhythm) and cognitive skills (executive functions, such as memory or attention).

Auditory deprivation and concomitant conditions, such as vestibular disorders, may affect the child's sensorimotor function, producing psychomotor developmental delays [2–5]. In this sense, psychomotor scores of hearing impaired (HI) children are poorer than those of normal hearing (NH) children [2, 6] and one third of HI children present retardation in motor outputs, such as head control or gait [7]. Although self-efficacy seems preserved [8], poor motor performance in HI children has been associated to less rich symbolic play, and difficulties in emotion adjustment and social peer interactions [6, 9]. In addition, procedures such as the cochlear implant may postpone gross motor function development for almost two years [10].

Fundamental motor skills include body perception, posture, coordination and gross and fine motor function.

Body perception perturbation might disturb the action-performance processes in HI children and be the origin many unexplained daily problems [11]. Posture is based in the perception of the body in the surrounding space and it is continuously adjusted to environmental variations by the permanent integration of multisensory inputs, such as vestibular, visual and proprioceptive information. The vestibular system, which can be damaged in HI children, provides the information of the head position and movements. Thus, HI children typically show less ample head movements and instable posture [3, 12], which try to compensate increasing the use of the other sensory inputs, mainly the visual ones [13]. This compensation makes possible the implementation of exercise programs for improving posture and balance control in HI children [14]. Stable posture adaptation to environmental conditions is closely interconnected with *balance*, a core substructure for higher gross motor skills, such as walking, standing on one leg, running or jumping [15]. HI children find difficulties to maintain balance control, as auditory information contributes to the mapping of the surrounding space by the creation of a hearing "map" [16, 17]. Thus, HI children have deficits in static and dynamic balance, characterized by faster and wider body sways, poor stability limits and higher energy expenditure for balance maintenance [18–21]. Vestibular deficits or cochlear implant surgery (which temporarily produces vestibular loss) are high-risk conditions for balance disturbance [19, 22–25] and inversely, balance deficits due to vestibular dysfunction have been identified as risk factors for cochlear implant failures [22]. Sensory compensation in situations of balance compromise, such as irregular surfaces, is used by HI children to reduce falls [20, 21]. In this context, vestibular rehabilitation and physical exercise, as well as hearing aids and exploitation of auditory mapping cues, may enhance vestibular adaptation and balance in HI children [16, 24, 26].

Coordination refers to the progressive contraction and relaxation of muscle groups, in a particular temporal sequence, to achieve a motor outcome. Auditory deprivation affects motion perception [27] and motor sequence learning [28], leading to a slowed-down motor development [29].

Thus, *fine motor function* or manipulation suffers a retardation along the years in prelingually HI children [28, 29] and gross motor functions requiring visuomotor, spatial and temporal coordination (e.g. catching a ball, running) are delayed in HI children compared to NH children [30]. In addition, HI children show atypical gross motor performance. For instance, their gait exhibits anomalous ground reaction forces, higher propulsion and lower free movements than that of NH children [18]. Visuomotor coordination seems to share brain networks with receptive and expressive language [29] and the level of auditory deprivation determine the accuracy of motor performance [18, 31]. In this sense, hearing aids and cochlear implants may help promote improvements in gross and fine motor function [17].

Perceptual motor skills include the concepts of space and time.

Spatial skills allow knowing object position and its relationship with the surrounding environment [32]. HI children compensate auditory deprivation with adaptation strategies, such as higher location memory [33], focus of attention to different stimuli in the different visual fields (i.e. central stimuli in far space and peripheral stimuli in near space) [34] or higher visual and tactile orientation in the allocentric frame of reference (encoding the position of an object in relation to others) [35]. These adaptation strategies seem unable to compensate actions based in the egocentric frame of reference (encoding the position of an object in relation to the own body), resulting in slower movement towards a goal [35]. Brain activation induced by spatial attention also appears to shift from the usual right hemisphere to be bilateral or located in the left hemisphere in HI children [33]. In addition, the lack of language results in a deficit in non-linguistic spatial cognition [36, 37]. For example, in deaf signers consistent linguistic markings of "left-right" or "ground" are related to searches under disorientation or in rotated arrays [36]. Spatial skills interventions, particularly with the use of sign language [38], have shown to be effective in HI children.

Time skills encompass the timing, order, sequence of stimuli and rhythm [39]. Auditory deprivation decreases the ability of using temporal cues for recognizing verbal and non-verbal signals out of the environmental noise [40] or the rhythm of oral or sign language [41]. Temporal processing of proprioceptive and tactile signals is also compromised in HI children [42]. Although time skills are harder to improve than spatial skills, an extended practice of the synchronization of temporally discrete visual stimuli and visual timing may promote cross-modal plasticity in HI children [43].

3 Systems to Train Psychomotor Skills

Mining the literature, we find different works dedicated to the design and development of interactive systems devoted to the psychomotor rehabilitation of children with hearing impairments. Researchers have used different technologies such as interactive floors, smartwatches or vision-based interfaces, to work these skills [44].

To practice body expression in order to enhance speech and language skills in HI children with cochlear implant, Iversen and Kortbek [45] developed an interactive floor based on body movements.

Computer vision techniques were also used to detect the children's body movements and use them to interact. Egusa et al. [46] built an application for HI children to express themselves by physical movement and to be able to interact in a puppet show. However, an evaluation was still needed with the end-users. Marnik et al. [47] developed a therapeutic and educational tool for children with developmental problems (which can include HI children). A narrator asked the children to perform an exercise or gesture, and their body movement detected by a Microsoft Kinect controlled an avatar. Conner et al. [48] also used a Microsoft Kinect to improve the body posture when performing physical exercises such as squats. The evaluation showed an improvement of the children's body posture when following the instructions of the system.

Radovanovic evaluated the visual-motor integration of 70 profoundly deaf children [49]. Results showed that all younger school-aged children from the experimental group (who played once a week for five months) showed better results on visual-motor tests after improving their visual-motor skills through the use of computer software on pcs.

To rehabilitate the upper body limbs, Wille et al. [50] built a VR environment and tested the system with children with motor impairments during three weeks. The system was not focused on HI children, but could be used to improve their skills.

Aditya et al. [51] proposed a system using a smartwatch to help children with learning disabilities to understand the concept of time. Instead of showing the time on the watch, they showed visuals, audio feedback and images from the daily life of children. Although the system is not focused specifically on HI children, they can benefit from it.

To train rhythm, we find different works using mobile devices to play rhythm games. These games aim at improving the visual motor skills of the HI children by motivating them to identify and produce rhythmic patterns [52, 53]. With the same aim in mind, other technologies had also been used such as tangible objects. Correa et al. [54] presented a piano which visualized and gave feedback of musical notes through visuals and vibrations. BoomChaCha is a rhythm-based, physical game where children interacted with tangible objects (e.g. waving weapons) [55]. By interacting with the system, children trained their body expression and body movements. The game was not designed specifically for HI children.

To improve HI children's sound localization acuity, Sogono and Richards [56] used theories on perceptual learning and perceptual motor training as a basis for developing training materials, which included multimodal and multisensory technologies. They provided a set of guidelines to develop this material.

4 Proposals for Interactive Systems for Rehabilitation

Based on the search for interactive systems aimed at the psychomotor rehabilitation of hearing impaired children, a series of physical and digital devices were identified that enrich the therapeutic activity and facilitate the achievement of the rehabilitation objective. Among the devices were body tracking systems, touch screens, cameras, sensors, electronic boards, interactive floors, audio systems, tangible and haptic devices.

Through this identification and understanding of the limitations of hearing impaired children in the development of psychomotor skills (cognitive, fundamental and perceptual), we propose the following interactive systems focused on the rehabilitation of fundamental skills and perceptual abilities.

4.1 Electronic Ping-Pong

This proposal is a racquet-shaped device that will allow the child to perform exercises to develop fundamental skills mainly hand-eye coordination and force management.

The function of this interaction device is that the child can bounce a small pin pong ball on the flat surface of the racket, which is divided into two zones a green and a yellow. The mechanics of the game is that each time the child bounces the ball, it must be done in one area at a time (green or yellow) simulating a game of pin pong. The ball cannot bounce more than once in the same area. Each time the child bounces the ball in the corresponding area this will give a point and will be shown on a small screen that is embedded in the surface of the racket. This device will have an Arduino Nano, piezoelectrics and LED screens that will allow to control and feedback the activity.

The goals of electronic ping pong are for the child to develop his perceptual motor skills (manual coordination, knowledge and identification of space and measurement of time and rhythm), attention skills, concentration, self-control, intrinsic self-evaluation, physical abilities, analysis, problem solving, strength estimation and rebound angles.

4.2   Storyteller Pencil

Interactive device based on artistic expression activities, with the aim of helping hearing impaired children to develop and rehabilitate their fundamental skills, mainly fine motor skills.

The idea of this interactive book is that in its pages will be representative drawings of different children's stories. This system invites the child to perform calligraphy tasks through the union of dots of the different drawings found in their pages. The moment the child finishes joining the dots of the image found on the sheet, the system displays through a screen a video of the story related to the image, in order to provide positive feedback for the successful completion of the activity.

The device is composed by a board, a pencil, computer and an Arduino to control the interaction; the board is adapted with terminal points of a matrix circuit, that is activated when connecting the different points of the drawing. For this a graphite pencil is used which is connected with a copper tip that allows to conduct small electric shocks, supplied by a battery; These electric shocks will go along the graphite path until the circle is closed. Once the dots of the figures are connected, an animation of a story is shown on the screen.

The activity proposed by the storyteller pencil allows the child to develop the motor perceptive ability, manual coordination, viso-motor perception, fine motor skills and symbolic ability.

4.3   Digital Labyrinth

Interactive device based on labyrinth games in which the child must solve the problem of choosing between different paths that may or may not lead to the goal or goal. The objective of this system is that the child can train his sense of spatiality and orientation.

The labyrinth will be built with foami material that will serve to indicate the path that the child must travel. It will also allow to mark the limits that will make the child not go out of the way or must decide at some point which path to take. The idea of the system is that it can be worked by levels, the first level will take the child to make the journey with the visual aid that will be shown through the use of LED lights incorporated in the foami slabs that build the road, the idea is that the child follows the path of the lights on to the finish line. In a second level the child must travel the road but this will no longer be indicated, only help will be given at the intersections showing an arrow direction that must recognize, at the time the child is placed in the tile, this will provide feedback by color depending on whether it is the right path or not. Finally, in a third level, the child should make the route without any help, only when it reaches the end of the system will make a positive visual feedback for their work well done.

The system will be built using foami slabs to build the different paths to the labyrinth. For the interaction with the foami slab, electric feet will be used to receive information about the pressure on the slab and to know when the child is on the slab. You can also add LED lights for visual feedback of the path or directions that the child should take at a given time, all this will be connected to an Arduino that will allow you to control the components and send data to the computer to make the visual reinforcement through the display screen.

The digital labyrinth will allow the child to develop his sense of orientation, recognition of space, coordination, balance, postural control and gait.

5 Conclusions

HI children, in addition to having difficulties in communication and language, also have deficits in their psychomotor skills which are important for the normal development of their emotions, actions and social activities. It is therefore important to contribute to the psychomotor development of this population.

The aim of this article was to enumerate the problems that HI's children have and to compile the efforts that are being made in the field to show which areas could be enriched with the use of interactive technologies and systems. This review shows that there is a lack of proposed tools to support these children during their therapy or education.

Therefore, this encourages us to actively participate in the generation of new interactive system proposals that enrich rehabilitation processes through more attractive and motivating tools for children with HI.

References

1. European Forum of Psychomotricity: Psychomotrician Professional Competences in Europe (2012)
2. Gheysen, F., Loots, G., Van Waelvelde, H.: Motor development of deaf children with and without cochlear implants. J. Deaf Stud. Deaf Educ. **13**, 215–224 (2008). https://doi.org/10.1093/deafed/enm053
3. Melo, R.d.S., Lemos, A., Macky, C.F.d.S.T., et al.: Postural control assessment in students with normal hearing and sensorineural hearing loss. Braz. J. Otorhinolaryngol. **81**, 431–438 (2015). https://doi.org/10.1016/j.bjorl.2014.08.014
4. Rajendran, V., Roy, F.G.: An overview of motor skill performance and balance in hearing impaired children. Ital. J. Pediatr. **37**, 33 (2011). https://doi.org/10.1186/1824-7288-37-33
5. Wiegersma, P.H., Velde, A.V.: Motor development of deaf children. J. Child Psychol. Psychiatry **24**, 103–111 (1983). https://doi.org/10.1111/j.1469-7610.1983.tb00107.x
6. Fellinger, M.J., Holzinger, D., Aigner, M., et al.: Motor performance and correlates of mental health in children who are deaf or hard of hearing. Dev. Med. Child Neurol. **57**, 942–947 (2015). https://doi.org/10.1111/dmcn.12814
7. Masuda, T., Kaga, K.: Relationship between acquisition of motor function and vestibular function in children with bilateral severe hearing loss. Acta Otolaryngol. **134**, 672–678 (2014). https://doi.org/10.3109/00016489.2014.890290
8. Engel-Yeger, B., Weissman, D.: A comparison of motor abilities and perceived self-efficacy between children with hearing impairments and normal hearing children. Disabil. Rehabil. **31**, 352–358 (2009). https://doi.org/10.1080/09638280801896548
9. Leigh, G., Ching, T.Y.C., Crowe, K., et al.: Factors affecting psychosocial and motor development in 3-year-old children who are deaf or hard of hearing. J. Deaf Stud. Deaf Educ. **20**, 331–342 (2015). https://doi.org/10.1093/deafed/env028

10. De Kegel, A., Maes, L., Van Waelvelde, H., Dhooge, I.: Examining the impact of cochlear implantation on the early gross motor development of children with a hearing loss. Ear Hear. **36**, e113–e121 (2015). https://doi.org/10.1097/AUD.0000000000000133
11. Houde, M.S., Landry, S.P., Page, S., et al.: Body perception and action following deafness. Neural Plast. (2016). https://doi.org/10.1155/2016/5260671
12. Melo, R.d.S.: Gait performance of children and adolescents with sensorineural hearing loss. Gait Posture **57**, 109–114 (2017). https://doi.org/10.1016/j.gaitpost.2017.05.031
13. An, M., Yi, C., Jeon, H., Park, S.: Age-related changes of single-limb standing balance in children with and without deafness. Int. J. Pediatr. Otorhinolaryngol. **73**, 1539–1544 (2009). https://doi.org/10.1016/j.ijporl.2009.07.020
14. Walowska, J., Bolach, B., Bolach, E.: The influence of Pilates exercises on body balance in the standing position of hearing impaired people. Disabil. Rehabil. 1–9 (2017). https://doi.org/10.1080/09638288.2017.1370731
15. Maes, L., De Kegel, A., Van Waelvelde, H., Dhooge, I.: Association between vestibular function and motor performance in hearing-impaired children. Otol. Neurotol. **35**, e343–e347 (2014)
16. Vitkovic, J., Le, C., Lee, S.L., Clark, R.A.: The contribution of hearing and hearing loss to balance control. Audiol. Neurotol. **21**, 195–202 (2016). https://doi.org/10.1159/000445100
17. Weaver, T.S., Shayman, C.S., Hullar, T.E.: The effect of hearing aids and cochlear implants on balance during gait. Otol. Neurotol. **38**, 1327–1332 (2017). https://doi.org/10.1097/MAO.0000000000001551
18. Melo, R.d.S., Marinho, S.E.d.S., Freire, M.E.A., et al.: Static and dynamic balance of children and adolescents with sensorineural hearing loss. Einstein (São Paulo) **15**, 262–268 (2017). https://doi.org/10.1590/s1679-45082017ao3976
19. Movallali, G., Ebrahimi, A.-A., Movallali, G., et al.: Balance performance of deaf children with and without cochlear implants. Acta Med. Iran **54**, 737–742 (2016)
20. Cai, Y., Zheng, Y., Liang, M., et al.: Auditory spatial discrimination and the mismatch negativity response in hearing-impaired individuals. PLoS ONE **10**, 1–18 (2015). https://doi.org/10.1371/journal.pone.0136299
21. Wolter, N.E., Cushing, S.L., Madrigal, L.D.V., et al.: Unilateral hearing loss is associated with impaired balance in children. Otol. Neurotol. **37**, 1589–1595 (2016). https://doi.org/10.1097/MAO.0000000000001218
22. Oyewumi, M., Wolter, N.E., Heon, E., et al.: Using balance function to screen for vestibular impairment in children with sensorineural hearing loss and cochlear implants. Otol. Neurotol. **37**, 926–932 (2016). https://doi.org/10.1097/MAO.0000000000001046
23. Zur, O., Shimron, H.B.-R., Leisman, G., Carmeli, E.: Balance versus hearing after cochlear implant in an adult. BMJ Case Rep. (2017). https://doi.org/10.1136/bcr-2017-220391
24. Parietti-Winkler, C., Lion, A., Montaut-Verient, B., et al.: Effects of unilateral cochlear implantation on balance control and sensory organization in adult patients with profound hearing loss. Biomed. Res. Int. (2015). https://doi.org/10.1155/2015/621845
25. Janky, K., Givens, D.: Vestibular, visual acuity and balance outcomes in children with cochlear implants: a preliminary report. Ear Hear. **36**, e364–e372 (2015). https://doi.org/10.1097/AUD.0000000000000194.Vestibular
26. Vidranski, T., Farkaš, D.: Motor skills in hearing impaired children with or without cochlear implant - a systematic review, 173–179 (2015)
27. Armstrong, B.A., Neville, H.J., Hillyard, S.A., Mitchell, T.V.: Auditory deprivation affects processing of motion, but not color. Cogn. Brain. Res. **14**, 422–434 (2002). https://doi.org/10.1016/S0926-6410(02)00211-2
28. Lévesque, J., Théoret, H., Champoux, F.: Reduced procedural motor learning in deaf individuals. Front. Hum. Neurosci. **8**, 343 (2014)

29. Horn, D.L., Fagan, M.K., Dillon, C.M., et al.: NIH public access. Sci. York 117, 2017–2025 (2008). https://doi.org/10.1097/MLG.0b013e3181271401
30. Savelsbergh, G., Netelenbos, J., Whiting, H.: Auditory perception and the control of spatially coordinated action of deaf and hearing impaired children. J. Child Psychol. Psychiatry 32, 489–500 (1991)
31. Greters, M.E., Bittar, R.S.M., Grasel, S.S., et al.: Desempenho auditivo como preditor de recuperação postural em usuários de implante coclear. Braz. J. Otorhinolaryngol. 83, 16–22 (2017). https://doi.org/10.1016/j.bjorl.2016.01.002
32. Conway, C.M., Kronenberger, W.G.: NIH public access. Medicine (Baltimore) 18, 275–279 (2010). https://doi.org/10.1111/j.1467-8721.2009.01651.x
33. Cattani, A., Clibbens, J.: Atypical lateralization of memory for location: effects of deafness and sign language use. Brain Cogn. 58, 226–239 (2005). https://doi.org/10.1016/j.bandc. 2004.12.001
34. Cattaneo, Z., Lega, C., Cecchetto, C., Papagno, C.: Auditory deprivation affects biases of visuospatial attention as measured by line bisection. Exp. Brain Res. 232, 2767–2773 (2014). https://doi.org/10.1007/s00221-014-3960-7
35. Zhang, M., Tan, X., Shen, L., et al.: Interaction between allocentric and egocentric reference frames in deaf and hearing populations. Neuropsychologia 54, 68–76 (2014). https://doi.org/ 10.1016/j.neuropsychologia.2013.12.015
36. Pyers, J.E., Shusterman, A., Senghas, A., et al.: Evidence from an emerging sign language reveals that language supports spatial cognition. Proc. Natl. Acad. Sci. 107, 12116–12120 (2010). https://doi.org/10.1073/pnas.0914044107
37. Gentner, D., Özyürek, A., Gürcanli, Ö., Goldin-Meadow, S.: Spatial language facilitates spatial cognition: evidence from children who lack language input. Cognition 127, 318–330 (2013). https://doi.org/10.1016/j.cognition.2013.01.003
38. Arnold, P., Mills, M.: Memory for faces, shoes, and objects by deaf and hearing signers and hearing nonsigners. J. Psycholinguist. Res. 30, 185–195 (2001). https://doi.org/10.1023/A: 1010329912848
39. Nava, E., Bottari, D., Zampini, M., Pavani, F.: Visual temporal order judgment in profoundly deaf individuals. Exp. Brain Res. 190, 179–188 (2008)
40. Moore, B.C.J.: The role of temporal fine structure processing in pitch perception, masking, and speech perception for normal-hearing and hearing-impaired people. JARO – J. Assoc. Res. Otolaryngol. 9, 399–406 (2008). https://doi.org/10.1007/s10162-008-0143-x
41. Colin, C., Zuinen, T., Bayard, C., Leybaert, J.: Phonological processing of rhyme in spoken language and location in sign language by deaf and hearing participants: a neurophysiological study. Neurophysiol. Clin. 43, 151–160 (2013). https://doi.org/10.1016/j.neucli.2013. 03.001
42. Bharadwaj, S.V., Matzke, P.L., Daniel, L.L.: Multisensory processing in children with cochlear implants. Int. J. Pediatr. Otorhinolaryngol. 76, 890–895 (2012). https://doi.org/10. 1016/j.ijporl.2012.02.066
43. Campos, P.D., Alvarenga, K.D.F., Frederigue, N.B., et al.: Temporal organization skills in cochlear implants recipients. Braz. J. Otorhinolaryngol. 74, 884–889 (2008). https://doi.org/ 10.1016/S1808-8694(15)30149-X
44. Peñeñory, V.M., Manresa-Yee, C., Riquelme, I., et al.: Scoping review of systems to train psychomotor skills in hearing impaired children. Sensors 18, 2546 (2018)
45. Iversen, O., Kortbek, K.: Stepstone: an interactive floor application for hearing impaired children with a cochlear implant. In: Proceedings of the 6th International Conference on Interaction Design and Children, Aalborg, Denmark, 6–8 June 2007, pp. 117–124 (2007)

46. Egusa, R., Wada, K., Namatame, M.: Development of an interactive puppet show system for the hearing-impaired people. In: Proceedings of the CONTENT 2012: The Fourth International Conference on Creative Content Technologies, Nice, France, 22–27 July 2012, pp. 69–71 (2012)

47. Marnik, J., Samolej, S., Kapu, T., Oszust, M., Wysocki, M.: Using computer graphics, vision and gesture recognition tools for building interactive systems supporting therapy of children. Hum. Comput. Syst. Interact. Backgrounds Appl. **2**, 539–553 (2012)

48. Conner, C.: Correcting exercise form using body tracking. In: Proceedings of the 2016 CHI Conference Extended Abstracts on Human Factors in Computing Systems, San Jose, CA, USA, 7–12 May 2016, pp. 3028–3034 (2016)

49. Radovanovic, V.: The influence of computer games on visual-motor integration in profoundly deaf children. Br. J. Spec. Educ. **40**, 182–188 (2013)

50. Wille, D., et al.: Virtual reality-based paediatric interactive therapy system (PITS) for improvement of arm and hand function in children with motor impairment—a pilot study. Dev. Neurorehabil. **12**, 44–52 (2009)

51. Aditya, V., Dhenki, S., Amarvaj, L., Karale, A., Singh, H.: Saathi: making it easier for children with learning disabilities to understand the concept of time. In: Proceedings of the 2016 CHI Conference Extended Abstracts on Human Factors in Computing Systems, San Jose, CA, USA, 7–12 May 2016, pp. 56–61 (2016)

52. Jouhtimäki, J., Kitunen, S., Plaisted, M., Rainò, P.: The brave little troll—a rhythmic game for deaf and hard of hearing children. In: Proceedings of the 13th International MindTrek Conference: Everyday Life in the Ubiquitous Era, Tampere, Finland, 30 September–2 October 2009

53. Pérez-Arévalo, C., Manresa-Yee, C., Beltrán, V.M.P.: Game to develop rhythm and coordination in children with hearing impairments. In: Proceedings of the XVIII International Conference on Human Computer Interaction, Cancun, Mexico, 25–27 September 2017

54. Correa, R.A., Osorio, A.: CASETO: Sistema Interactivo Basado en Sinestesia Para La Enseñanza/Aprendizaje De La Música Para Niños Con Discapacidad Auditiva Entre 7 a 11 Años. Editorial Bonaventuriana—Universidad Autonoma de Occidente. Obras colectivas en ciencias de la computación, pp. 37–52 (2017). ISBN 978-958-5415-19-5

55. Zhu, F., Sun, W., Zhang, C., Ricks, R.: BoomChaCha. In: Proceedings of the 2016 CHI Conference Extended Abstracts on Human Factors in Computing Systems, San Jose, CA, USA, 7–12 May 2016, pp. 184–187 (2016)

56. Sogono, M.C., Richards, D.: A design template for multisensory and multimodal games to train and test children for sound localisation acuity. In: Proceedings of the 9th Australasian Conference Interact Entertain Matters Life Death, Melbourne, Australia, 30 September–1 October 2013, pp. 1–10 (2013)

Spatio-Temporal Gait Analysis Based on Human-Smart Rollator Interaction

Atia Cortés[1]([✉]) [iD], Antonio B. Martínez[2] [iD], and Javier Béjar[1] [iD]

[1] KEMLg, Universitat Politecnica de Catalunya - Barcelona Tech,
Barcelona, Spain
{acortes,bejar}@cs.upc.edu
[2] GRINS, Universitat Politecnica de Catalunya - Barcelona Tech,
Barcelona, Spain
antonio.b.martinez@upc.edu
https://kemlg.upc.edu/en

Abstract. The ability to walk is typically related to several biomechanical components that are involved in the gait cycle (or stride), including free mobility of joints, particularly in the legs; coordination of muscle activity in terms of timing and intensity; and normal sensory input, such as vision and vestibular system. As people age, they tend to slow their gait speed, and their balance is also affected. Also, the retirement from the working life and the consequent reduction of physical and social activity contribute to the increased incidence of falls in older adults. Moreover, older adults suffer different kinds of cognitive decline, such as dementia or attention problems, which also accentuate gait disorders and its consequences. In this paper we present a methodology for gait identification using the on-board sensors of a smart rollator: the *i-Walker*. This technique provides the number of steps performed in walking exercises, as well as the time and distance travelled for each stride. It also allows to extract spatio-temporal metrics used in medical gait analysis from the interpretation of the interaction between the individual and the *i-Walker*. In addition, two metrics to assess users' driving skills, laterality and directivity, are proposed.

Keywords: Assistive Technologies · Healthcare · Gait analysis

1 Introduction

In nowadays greying society, a large amount of people require appropriated and personalized assistance, This circumstance leaves room for new technologies that offer this population an extraordinary opportunity to perform their activities of daily living (ADL) and to improve their autonomy. Of all world regions, Europe has the highest proportion of population aged 65 or over, a statistic that becomes more pessimistic according to the baseline projection of Eurostat, which shows that this percentage will almost double to more than 25% in the year 2050 [17].

H. M. Fardoun et al. (Eds.): REHAB 2016, CCIS 1002, pp. 68–83, 2019.
https://doi.org/10.1007/978-3-030-16785-1_6

In addition, in this population sector the frequency of falls increases with age and frailty level. These to factors are a main cause of unintentional injury, due to a combination of biological factors and disease-related conditions. This has several implications in the Quality of Life (QoL) of the elderly: the more they reduce their ADLs, the more their frailty and fear of falling increases, losing their residual skills as a consequence. This will represent a challenge for the public health systems that will have to face a huge economic impact to deal with this demographic situation. This is not sustainable in certain countries and it is already a world-wide issue.

Assistive Technologies (AT) play a key role in providing solutions to improve the QoL of this target population. Furthermore, one of the main objectives for the European Union H2020 programme has been to focus on the analysis of the causes and consequences of pathologies in order to find patterns that will support early detection of a disease or associated risks. Consequently, the care community could take decisions on preventive intervention and educational information in order to delay the physical or cognitive decline of the elderly and try to keep them independent as long as possible living in the community. The evolution of ICT tools in collaboration with medical knowledge has empowered the use of sensorized assistive devices that can provide ubiquitous, real-time information about a person's evolution in terms of physical and cognitive conditions.

In this paper we introduce a set of metrics to assess gait quality and risk of falling in elderly individuals using a smart rollator: the *i-Walker* [6]. The aim is to identify significant characteristics, providing in a future a decision support tool to clinicians and caregivers for walking assessment and user profiling.

1.1 Plan of Work

In Sect. 2 the context in which the *i-Walker* was used to collect the data from a group of elderly people is detailed. Section 3 introduces a set of definitions and representations that will be used to measure users' performance while using the *i-Walker*. Section 4 explains the methodology applied to the signals collected from the sensors of the walker to extract gait information. In Sect. 5 some results from the data collected from two groups of elder adults are depicted. Finally Sect. 6 provides some conclusions and future work.

2 Components of the Study

This section describes the different components that were used to carry on the study here presented: the measurement tool, the *i-Walker*, the participants and the type of exercises that were performed.

2.1 Measurement Tool: The *i-Walker*

Assistive devices are developed to help in the daily lives of elderly and disabled people. The *i-Walker* is based on a standard 4-wheeled rollator with embedded sensors and actuators. Its aim is to provide mobility support and rehabilitation to persons with a physical and/or cognitive disability, as well as to monitor their activities. It has a distributed micro-controller architecture which drives the system and records and provides information to clinicians (see Fig. 1):

1. *Handlers* contain force sensors which measure pushing, leaning and lateral forces (X, Y and Z axis respectively) on both hands. They also have a multicoloured lighting ring (5) used to indicate different states of the *i-Walker* to the user, like calibration status and battery level.
2. *Rear wheels* embed motors that work as actuators, the purpose is to supply a set of operative modes which provide pushing or pulling help depending on the control strategy.
3. *Central box* under the seat contains the computing power on-board (*e.g.* a Raspberry Pi) and a set of sensors that will provide information about movement and tilt.
4. *Blocking brakes* are situated in the rear legs and provide a braking help when the *i-Walker* detects the user is driving in downhill. For safety reasons the *i-Walker* automatically stops when the user releases the handlers, that is, when no forces are detected on them.

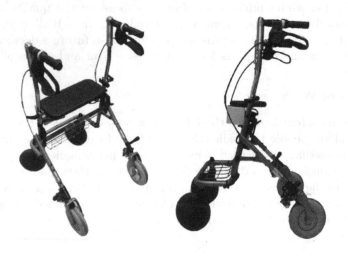

Fig. 1. The *i-Walker*

For each exercise or activity that users perform with the *i-Walker*, data from each sensor is recorded every 100 ms and stored in the Raspberry Pi as individual time series. From its on-board sensors, the *i-Walker* can infer the travelled distance, the walking time, the maximal speed, the maximum of the lateral deviation and the force exerted individually in both handlebars. Moreover, after processing the signals, it is possible to obtain specific information of the user's walking behaviour at a given moment of the exercise, being either in terms of distance or time in the trajectory, a concrete step number or by maxima speed or force.

2.2   Walking Tests

The 10 Metre Walking Test (10MWT) is a performance measure used in rehabilitation to assess walking speed over a short distance. It can be employed to determine functional mobility, gait and vestibular function [1].

During a 10MWT exercise, the subject has to walk 10 m in a maximal straight way. This is traditionally measured with a stopwatch in terms of the time duration and the resulting average speed of the participant. The first and last two metres, that are related to the acceleration and deceleration phases, are discarded and only the central part of the exercise is taken into account, where it is assumed that the walking speed is almost constant. It is considered that gait speed can be a useful outcome to assess the physical decline of elderly people as well as to predict the risk of falling, other health deterioration or even survival [8]. Gait velocity has been related with the ageing process, although results are uncertain due to biological and behavioural differences among the population [13].

Another commonly used metric is the 6 Minutes Walking Test (6mWT), which assesses endurance in older adults by measuring the walked distance in that time. In terms of gait analysis and walking behaviour patterns, this measure should be more relevant since it provides more knowledge about each individual. For this study, it was decided to reduce this walking time to only three minutes following the clinical team indications. Thus, the participants walked in a 40-metres indoor corridor during three minutes. When the end of the corridor was reached, they turned back and walked to the starting point. Afterwards, the turning phases were excluded in the pre-processing step, storing each straight line as a single exercise. Moreover, in order to be compliant with the 10MWT exercise, the initial and final 20% were excluded. Then the average walking speed is calculated for the central 60% of the exercise. Consequently, bounds are recalculated, keeping the piece of exercise that starts and ends at this average walking speed.

2.3   Participants

Our initial target population consists of older adults, aged 65+ years old, with a good cognitive condition (MMSE > 23) and having suffered a previous fall in the last year or being considered as a person with high risk of falling (Tinetti Scale < 21 [14]). Individuals with any diagnosed mental disorder, such as dementia, or bearers of implantable electronic devices were excluded. Participants involved in this study come from residential care centres and hospitals from Italy and Spain and are divided in two different groups.

Table 1. Participants' age and gender distribution for each pilot. Each column represents a pilot.

Pilot	IDF (N = 85)	MAD (N = 59)	CVI (N = 41)
Age range			
Y	0 (0%)	0 (0%)	17 (41%)
M	35 (41%)	8 (13%)	9 (21%)
O	50 (59%)	51 (87%)	16 (38%)
Age			
Mean (± SD)	82.7 (± 8.3)	87.6 (± 5.8)	64.1 (± 23.1)
Min	65	70	22
Max	97	96	94
Gender			
F	58 (68%)	37 (63%)	34 (81%)
M	27 (32%)	22 (37%)	8 (19%)
Gait velocity	**T0/T1**		
Low	52/50	34	8
Medium	27/22	20	17
High	6/12	4	16
Tinetti	**T0/T1**		
Low	8/11	2	25
Medium	30/46	20	9
High	47/28	37	8

The first group is composed by 85 participants of the European funded project *I-DONT FALL* (*IDF* from now on, [7]), which has already been introduced in previous works [3,4]. In addition, data from another 60 participants from a care centre in Madrid (*MAD*) involved in the *IDF* project were collected following similar inclusion and exclusion criteria. People in this first group performed the 10MWT in an indoor corridor twice. In the case of *IDF*, data was collected before and after a three months training program (T0 and T1 periods respectively), where participants were assigned to a physical, cognitive, mixed or placebo group. The aim was to prove the effectiveness of a fall prevention system by observing the reduction of the incidence of falls, along with the risk and fear of falling. The *MAD* group performed two 10MWT exercises on a same session. After excluding drop-outs and some cases of sensor failure, this group was composed by 285 10MWT exercises.

The second group of participants was composed by 41 residents and workers of the Centre de Vida Independent (CVI), a care centre in Barcelona, and included people with a wider age range, under 65 years and with no previous fall. The objective was to observe differences in terms of walking behaviours among the different age groups. In this case, participants performed the 3mWT in a 40 m indoor corridor, since it is able to offer a more complete profile of each user. After the data cleaning process, where the turning areas are excluded and each straight line is considered as a single exercise, this group is represented by 153 instances.

Table 1 shows the representation of the participants in each pilot by *(i)* age <65 years (Y), 65–80 (M), 85> (O); *(ii)* gender (Female and Male); *(iii)* risk of falling based on the Tinetti scale (Low, Medium, High) and *(iv)* gait velocity, or GV (Low, Medium, High). This last metric is categorised based on [8], where authors determine that the walking speed is a relevant indicator to predict adverse events in healthy elders. Moreover, in [9], authors relate the walking speed to physical and medical status of older adults. In particular, individuals walking under 0.6 m/s (belonging to the Low gait velocity group) are considered people at high risk of falling, along with a high probability of developing comorbidities. People walking at a gait velocity higher than 1 m/s are categorised as High gait velocity and the rest fall in the Medium group.

3 Definition of Metrics

There are several methods for evaluating the human-robot interaction while driving. In our case, the *i-Walker* works with a purely reactive control and does not provide any supporting help to the user while driving. Thus, it will only act as a sensing platform that collects data during the exercise at a rate of 10 Hz. This work focuses on the information generated from the force sensors embedded on the handles and the odometry calculated from wheel encoders.

3.1 Spatio-Temporal Characteristics

The ability to walk normally is related to several biomechanical components involved in the gait cycle (or stride), which is composed of the stance and swing phases. The faster we walk, the shorter the stance phase will be. Usually, when talking about walking analysis, users' performances are assessed in terms of gait quality and gate associated disturbances caused by ageing, but also to cognitive and/or physical disabilities. Different approaches on the assessment of gait quality have been proposed with different perspectives: anthropometric, spatio-temporal, kinetic or kinematic (a complete review is offered in [12]).

Gait analysis is often carried on in controlled environments, such as especial rooms with cameras that are used to identify steps or by using wearable sensors on participants. Spatio-temporal parameters provide the simplest form of objective gait evaluation in terms of time and distance. These parameters have often been used to study the relation between gait quality and cognition in older adults [9]. This paper presents a technique that uses the information extracted by the interaction of the user with the *i-Walker*, and thus with its sensors. The stride duration is measured in terms of time and distance and then related to the amount of pushing force exerted at each moment. Force sensors will not only allow to shape driving skills, but are also able to provide a qualitative spatio-temporal assessment. For each exercise, the interpretation of the *i-Walker* sensor data is able to provide the following metrics:

- walked time and distance (in seconds and metres respectively),
- average walking speed or gait velocity (m/s),
- number of strides,
- stride length distance (in metres) of a gait cycle (or the time between steps of the same foot),
- stride time duration (in seconds) of a gait cycle (or the time between steps of the same foot),
- cadence (strides/minute or the number of strides * 60/walked time), and
- average pushing force (Newtons) of the force shape extracted from each stride.

In this work, the stride length and time will be considered as the average value of the whole exercise, in addition to its standard deviation and covariance. These two parameters will define the gait variability of each user, which is also a useful indicator of gait dysfunction.

3.2 User Driving Skills

There are several methods of evaluating the human-robot interaction while driving. In [15], the author proposes methods to *(i)* analyse user driving skills and obtain user profiles according to their performance, and *(ii)* interpret user disagreement in a collaborative control driving strategy.

For this work, we have defined two different evaluation metrics, laterality and directivity, which measure the ability to walk directly to an objective and with small oscillations in a straight line. It will also provide information on how balanced are user's movements and force load to the *i-Walker* in relation to the deviation angle. These deviations are being considered as lateral errors and occur when the user is not driving on the desired path. These lateral errors are calculated in terms of areas (m^2). The smaller the area is, the better the driving ability. However, in a controlled exercise like the 10MWT (which is usually performed in a corridor), deviations are expected to be relatively small (less than 50 cm).

The first term that we have defined is the Laterality of the trajectory. Based on the 10MWT, where the user is supposed to follow a straight line but only having the starting and ending point markers as path indicators, the Laterality measures the area between the starting point and user's ending point in relation to the predetermined ending point (the final goal). An ideal straight line would always show values around zero in the Y-axis, while the X-axis would increment with the travelled distance. This metric is obtained by adding the absolute value of the area generated by the Y-axis for each increment in X-axis. In addition, this metric allows to assess body force compensation, or balance, by measuring the areas of the trajectory on the right or left side of the desired destination.

The second term defined is the Directivity of the user. Given the user's trajectory and his/her ending point (not the original goal, but the new one determined by the orientation of his/her path), we calculate how straight did he/she go to that final destination. The estimated straight line that the user is following according to his original deviation is calculated using a least squares linear regression. Not only are we representing how straight did the user go to the predetermined destination point, but also how balanced was the user's navigation, *i.e.* did the user drive on the left or right side of a straight (imaginary) line. The estimated line is rotated to have zero Y-axis values. Therefore, dimensions of the areas are proportional to this projection of the linear regression. Even though there are other possibilities to measure this metric, this rotation was made to simplify the visualisation of the areas of deviation in terms of a straight line (*i.e.* to simulate the ideal case where the user would follow a perfectly straight line).

4   Methodology

In this work, we propose a methodology for gait cycle (or stride) identification based on the interaction of the user with the *i-Walker* through the force sensors embedded in the handlers. A first proposal of this methodology was presented in [4] using the 10MWT exercises. Other researchers have also used robotic rollators and/or other automatic means to measure users' performance in the 10MWT. For instance, in [16], authors propose a methodology to identify steps in straight line exercises using the angular velocity. This is used to determine the swaying phase of the gait cycle when the angular velocity has zero-value. A previous methodology using the *i-Walker* was proposed in [2] using the pushing force inputs to identify gait cycles. The study was applied to a group of geriatric users with different ambulatory problems, including individuals with leg amputations. There are other approaches for gait analysis that are not using any support device, but instead use visual tools to identify steps: in [18], authors use a laser range sensor in order to track leg movements in a controlled indoor scenario; recorded kinematic data from infra-red cameras is used in [10].

It has been observed that people, and especially women, present a hip sway during the swing phase in order to balance the weight. When using a rollator, this swaying is accompanied by a pushing force coming from the arm that will allow to move it from one point to another. Hence, we can extract the movements of the individual through the *i-Walker* by using its force sensors. As shown in Fig. 2 (top), left and right hand pushing forces are opposed, *i.e.* when one signal increases, generally the second decreases. It is then possible to interpret the number of steps performed during an exercise by using the following formula:

$$F_x diff = rhfx - lhfx$$

where $rhfx$ corresponds to the right hand pushing force and $lhfx$ is the left hand pushing force. In Fig. 2 (bottom) positive values on the resulting signal F_xdiff are those where the right hand was exerting a higher pushing force than the left hand, and thus corresponds to the steps performed by the right foot.

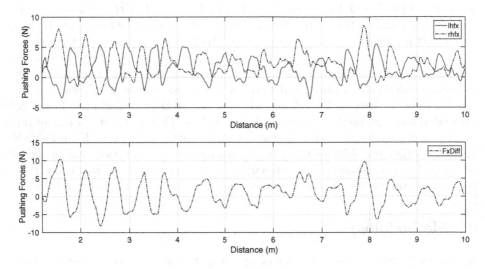

Fig. 2. (top) Hand pushing force on each handlebar; (bottom) Resulting pushing vector obtained with F_xDiff

The peaks of the signal are interpreted as gait cycles, where positive values will correspond to the right foot strides and negative values will be related to left foot strides. However, the signal needs to be filtered in order to discard smaller peaks that could be mistakenly considered as a step. The `findpeaks` function in MATLAB allows to identify peaks by local maxima along with different filtering options. In [4], peaks were extracted by a minimum height filter, also called prominence, based on the pushing force exerted. However, `findpeaks` allows also to filter by minimum distance between peaks, where distance can be either a time measure or other specified in the parameters. In this case, signals were filtered by a minimum of walked distance between strides based on the average walking speed. Figure 3 shows the final peaks considered right strides after the filtering process. Working with time series, allows to associate each peak to a moment in the exercise in terms of time and walked distance. Thus, it is possible to easily extract the spatio-temporal characteristics above mentioned for each stride and for each exercise.

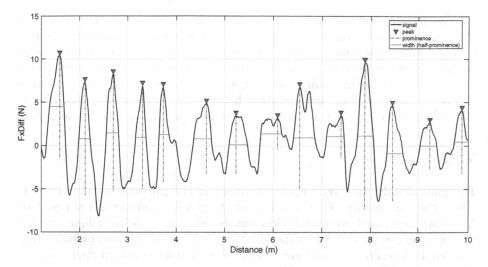

Fig. 3. Right leg strides, pushing force increments and average pushing time within peaks

As above said, the positive parts of the signal correspond to those moments where the user was exerting more force with its right hand. It is expected that in an exercise like the 10MWT, where the trajectory is assumed to be a straight line, the $F_x diff$ signal will be balanced: a person drifting to one side while driving will present less zero-time moments, since the increasings in the opposite side will not be high enough to compensate the movement. The observation of the force shape applied during the exercise illustrates the walking behaviour of each individual, *i.e.*, how does the individual interact with the *i-Walker* and associate it with a possible physical or cognitive dysfunction.

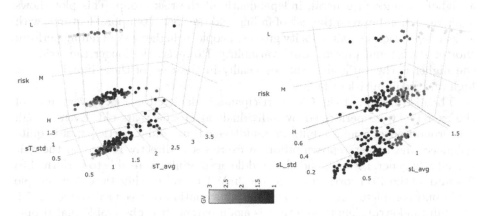

Fig. 4. IDFMAD dataset represented in terms of risk of falling and gait velocity groups. (a) Stride time and standard deviation; (b) stride length and standard deviation

The pushing force shape represented in Fig. 3 shows that the participant starts with a secure, constant walking speed but at some point changes the pattern and presents several irregularities. This type of observations allows to relate the quality of the walking pattern with the risk of falling or other health conditions affecting the older adult. Moreover, with a larger set of profiles, it could be useful to identify walking patterns that have already been defined according to different ageing characteristics (*e.g.* cautious gait, propulsive gait or atasia [11]).

5   Results

The gait identification technique introduced in the previous section allows to assess the gait quality of our participants from a spatio-temporal perspective. As before mentioned, we have divided our population by risk of falling and gait velocity. Figures 4 and 5 depict the distribution of the individuals by stride time and length in each pilot and are compared with their standard deviation, *i.e.* how regular is their pace along the exercise.

Figure 4 represents the IDF and MAD population, were most of the participants had already previous falls or high risk of falling. The distribution in terms of gait velocity is coherent with the risk of falling, since most of the people with high GV belong to the Low risk group. In fact, people in the Low risk group are in general those individuals who better recovered after the 3-months training period in IDF project. The left plot shows that this group is the one with shorter strides in time and higher gait velocity, while the other two risk groups present more variety in results. In addition we observe that the higher the risk of falling is, the more significant is also the standard deviation on time, which is almost proportional to the stride time. This can be interpreted as a sign of irregular pace, which might be due to several stops in the path or an indicator of insecurity. This pattern is also observable in the right side plot, where the stride length is represented. In this case, the distribution of stride length depicts a higher variance in general, independently of the risk group. This plot shows again a relation between the risk of falling and the spatio temporal features, with a clear separation by gait velocity groups. People at higher risk of falling perform shorter strides and present lower variability. However, the longer the stride is, the higher is the variability too, especially in the case of these individuals at high and medium risk of falling.

The distribution of the CVI participants is depicted in Fig. 5, were most of the exercises were performed by individuals aged <65 years old. Even though the proportion of young adults *vs* middle-aged and older participants is quite balanced, the higher representation in exercises is directly related to the gait velocity. In general, young and also middle-aged adults were able to perform 4 to 6 rounds of the 40 m corridor during the 3mWT exercise, while the elderly people could only complete 2 rounds in average. The relation between gait velocity, risk of falling and stride length and time is again patent. It is observable that people at high risk and low gait velocity perform shorter strides in length but longer in time. It is also surprising the number of exercises performed by young adults

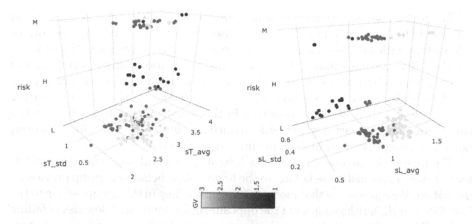

Fig. 5. CVI dataset represented in terms of risk of falling and gait velocity groups. (a) Stride time and standard deviation; (b) stride length and standard deviation

that belong to the second GV group. We were able also to observe that people who have never used a rollator before tend to modify their walking pace and behaviour.

Figure 5 shows that people with low and medium risk of falling are very disperse in terms of stride time. Healthy participants perform longer strides but with a variability of up to one metre. Older individuals with high risk of falling and low gait velocity tend to me more regular in their stride length, but have also an irregular pace. This is probably related to a cautious gait, usually present in geriatric population and sign of fear of falling. We have assumed that gait variability is higher in this dataset due to the length of the exercise, where the fatigue of walking for several minutes is latent in the obtained distribution.

Finally, if we observe the values in the average stride time in both pilots, we can observe that those in Fig. 4 have a larger range of values, going from 0.5 to 3.5 s while in Fig. 5 these go from 2 to 4 s. Values in stride length are more similar, although in the case of IDFMAD pilot there is a bigger group of individuals walking under 0.5 m/s. This could be helpful to determine different profiles of walking patterns, in which challenged older adults presenting high cadence are performing significantly short strides but in a considerable time, making their ambulation unstable.

In terms of driving skills, results show three main walking behaviours:

- Good laterality and directivity: people who drives around the desired straight line, presenting low oscillations around this trajectory
- Bad laterality, good directivity: individuals that present a deviation and keep this direction during the whole exercise.
- Bad laterality, bad directivity: this scenario presents different situations. In general it represents exercises where the user starts driving to the desired destination but at some point deviates its target goal and changes orientation. Other cases depict multiple changes or corrections of orientation during the exercise.

Since the exercises where performed in indoor scenarios, the most common walking behaviour is the first one, where users where able to maintain a correct orientation with small oscillations, probably due to the swaying movement while walking. The second walking behaviour shows deviations up to 4 m from the original final point and are in general deviations to the left. This pattern depicts a lack of body force compensation, where people tend to apply more forces from the right side of the body and resulting in this left deviation. Individuals in the third group are those with worse performance in terms of driving skills. However, not all of them belong to high or medium risk of falling.

Figure 6 shows that people with low lateral error has also in general low directivity error. These instances belong to the first walking behaviour group previously described. We can observe that most of the people falling in this group belong to the Low GV and High risk groups. On the opposite, older adults with low risk of falling and walking at high velocity are those with worse driving performances in proportion to the number of instances. The medium risk group is also quite disperse. There are several instances in these two groups with high values of laterality, but mild to moderate directivity errors, whom belong to the second walking behaviour group. It is assumable that people who walk faster also apply larger forces to the *i-Walker* and thus, the laterality decompensation becomes more patent. A more continued testing would be necessary to determine if this pattern is an early detector of physical or cognitive decline in elderly people.

The most critical case is the one representing the third walking behaviour, where not only the lack of body balance is latent, but also the ability to orientate and maintain a given direction. We can observe some instances in the High risk of falling group and in general in the individuals with Low GV distributed in the other risk of falling groups. It is interesting to observe the resulting trajectory

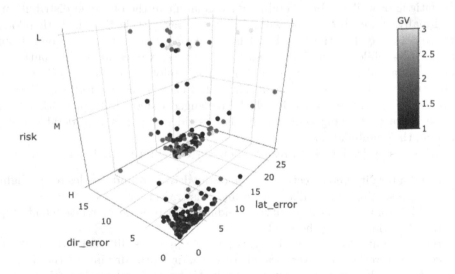

Fig. 6. Relation of the Laterality and Directivity driving skills of the IDFMAD users

of these instances. People with worst directivity results are those that present multiple oscillations along the exercise, even though the laterality is quite maintained (the trajectory is deviated up to 60 cm approximatively). This walking behaviour corresponds to individuals with a cautious and slow gait who are not able to maintain a continuous pace, but instead pauses after each step in order to change the body force from one side to the other.

6   Conclusion and Future Work

Demographic statistics show how the elderly population keeps growing as well as their demands. Meeting their needs presents important technical, social and economic challenges. As elderly individuals move toward higher levels of care (*i.e.*, from independent living to assisted living facilities to nursing homes), costs increase while their quality of life rapidly decreases. Assistive Technologies play a key role in nowadays society, since they not only focus on older adults but can also assist younger individuals with some kind of physical or cognitive impairment.

The *i-Walker* provides a better understanding of loading and force distribution for weight support and balance enhancement among users while providing mobility assistance at the same time. In this paper, an approach on spatio-temporal analysis is presented using only the information obtained through the interaction of the participants with the force sensors embedded on the *i-Walker*'s handlers. Results show a significant difference in gender, where usually men tend to walk faster and with larger stride length, which is coherent with the anthropometric characteristics. Moreover, there is a relation among age, risk of falling and gait variability. In particular, people performing the walking test at a low cadence, with short and slow strides, are those presenting a higher variance, especially in terms of stride time. Thus, the methodology is able to identify those individuals at higher risk of falling or developing other comorbidities. The results obtained are coherent with those found in literature, where gait velocity and cadence are dependent of the gender and age, but also to the risk of falling.

The *i-Walker'* sensor data is also able to generate profiles based on the driving skills of older adults, *e.g.* if they tend to deviate from their target destination, which can be related to a body force decompensation and, thus, to other early indicators of cognitive decline. A clinical expert should determine which of the walking behaviours above presented is more significant for early detection of decline symptoms: either the lack of orientation or body compensation are clear indicators of dysfunction. A relation between the spatio-temporal parameters and the driving skills has also emerged and presented in [5], where strides are compared based on the force shape obtained with $F_x diff$ and grouped by similarity using unsupervised learning methods.

Introducing younger participants to our study was useful to confirm this relation, but we consider that this demographic group should not be included in future works. In fact, people that have never used a rollator before tend to modify their walking behaviour, both in terms of gait velocity and force interaction, and might lead to false classifications. An in depth study using specific target pathologies, *e.g.* frailty or vascular dementia should be necessary in order to further generalize results. Moreover, it could be interesting to add new tools such as a Kinect or video camera in order to verify the sensitivity of the presented methodology.

The main benefit of using sensorized devices is that they are able to provide objective data to clinicians instead of relying on diagnoses obtained by observation, which is the traditional method of physical assessment. By complementing the clinical knowledge with sensor data information, it is expected to design decision support tools able to assist clinicians in the diagnose or rehabilitation treatment, but also to predict the risk of falling in senior population or the development of other commorbidities.

References

1. Adell, E., Wehmhörner, S., Rydwik, E.: The test-retest reliability of 10 meters maximal walking speed in older people living in a residential care unit. J. Geriatr. Phys. Ther. **36**(2), 74–77 (2013)
2. Ballesteros, J., Urdiales, C., Martinez, A.B., Tirado, M.: Automatic assessment of a rollator-user's condition during rehabilitation using the i-Walker platform. IEEE Trans. Neural Syst. Rehabil. Eng. **25**(11), 2009–2017 (2017)
3. Cortés, A., et al.: A fall prevention protocol using the i-Walker robotic rollator: the I-DONT-FALL project. In: 14th International Conference on Mobility and Transport for Elderly and Disabled Persons, TRANSED 2015, Lisbon, Portugal, pp. 1366–1380 (2015)
4. Cortés, A., Martínez, A.B., Béjar, J. (eds.): 4th Workshop on ICTs for Improving Patients Rehabilitation Research Techniques, REHAB 2016. ACM, New York (2016)
5. Cortés, A., Ojeda, M., Béjar, A.B., Martínez, J.: An approach to gait analysis from human-rollator interaction: the i-Walker. In: 21th International Conference of the Catalan Association for Artificial Intelligence, 8–10 October 2018, Spain (2018)
6. Cortés, U., Martínez-Velasco, A., Barrué, C., Annicchiarico, R.: AI based fall management services - the role of the i-Walker in I-DONTFALL. In: Advances in Artificial Intelligence - 11th Mexican International Conference on Artificial Intelligence, MICAI 2012, San Luis Potosí, Mexico, 2012, pp. 395–406 (2012)
7. Integrated prevention and Detection sOlutioNs Tailored to the population and Risk Factors associated with FALLs. http://www.idontfall.eu/ (2010)
8. Montero-Odasso, M., et al.: Gait velocity as a single predictor of adverse events in healthy seniors aged 75 years and older. J. Gerontol. Ser. A: Biol. Sci. Med. Sci. **60**(10), 1304–1309 (2005)
9. Montero-Odasso, M., Verghese, J., Beauchet, O., Hausdorff, J.M.: Gait and cognition: a complementary approach to understanding brain function and the risk of falling. J. Am. Geriatr. **60**(11), 2127–2136 (2012)
10. Nooijen, C., ter Hoeve, N., Field-Fote, E.: Gait quality is improved by locomotor training in individuals with SCI regardless of training approach. J. NeuroEng. Rehabil. **6**, 36 (2009)
11. Pirker, W., Katzenschlager, R.: Gait disorders in adults and the elderly. Wiener Klinische Wochenschrift **129**(3–4), 81–95 (2017)

12. Prakash, C., Kumar, R., Mittal, N.: Recent developments in human gait research: parameters, approaches, applications, machine learning techniques, datasets and challenges. Artif. Intell. Rev. **49**, 1–40 (2016)
13. Shimada, H., et al.: Physical factors underlying the association between lower walking performance and falls in older people: a structural equation model. Arch. Gerontol. Geriatr. **53**(2), 131–134 (2010)
14. Tinetti, M.E., Speechley, M., Ginter, S.F.: Risk factors for falls among elderly persons living in the community. New Engl. J. Med. **319**(26), 1701–1707 (1988)
15. Urdiales, C.: Collaborative Assistive Robot for Mobility Enhancement (CARMEN) - The Bare Necessities: Assisted Wheelchair Navigation and Beyond. Vol. 27 of Intelligent Systems Reference Library. Springer, Heidelberg (2012). https://doi.org/10.1007/978-3-642-24902-0
16. Wang, T., et al.: Walking analysis of young and elderly people by using an intelligent walker ANG. Robot. Auton. Syst. (2014)
17. WHO: European health report 2012: charting the way to well-being. World Health Organization (2013)
18. Yorozu, A., Moriguchi, T., Takahashi, M.: Improved leg tracking considering gait phase and spline-based interpolation during turning motion in walk tests. Sensors **15**(9), 22451 (2015)

Design and Implementation of Internet of Things and Cloud Based Platform for Remote Health Monitoring and Fall Detection

Ala' F. Khalifeh[1(✉)], Adham Saleh[1], Mahmoud AL-Nuimat[1],
Dhiah el Diehn I. Abou-Tair[1], and Nasim Alnuman[2]

[1] School of Electrical Engineering and IT, German-Jordanian University,
Amman, Jordan
ala.khalifeh@gju.edu.jo
[2] The School of Applied Medical Sciences, Amman, Jordan

Abstract. With the proliferation of the Internet of Things (IoT) and cloud computing technologies in various fields, remote health monitoring and fall detection are two vital applications that are expected to adopt these technologies. This is due to the fact that it not only provides efficient way for logging the patients' health information, thus providing an electronic record for all the vital health signs that the patient is monitoring utilizing various medical IoT devices, but also it can be used to send an alert message to the healthcare personnel in case of detecting any abnormal behavior hence providing an immediate assistance. Fall detection is another important application of these technologies, where wearable sensors can be used to send an alert message to the healthcare personnel in case of detecting unpredicted fall. In this book chapter, the design and implementation of a simple and cost effective healthcare monitoring and fall detection system that utilizes of-the-shelf electronic components is provided. The system consists of a microcontroller, medical sensors and communication module that are used to collect the patients' information and send it to the cloud for further processing and analysis. Furthermore, a fall detection system that utilizes wearable sensors is proposed where it can detect unpredicted fall. One unique feature in this system that it utilizes voice recognition technology to interact with the patient after detecting a fall, thus verifying if the patient needs an assistant or not, which in turn reduces the false alarms and improves the system accuracy.

Keywords: E-health · Medical sensors · Microcontroller · Cloud computing · Remote monitoring · Fall detection · Voice recognition

1 Introduction

The advent of new technologies has reshaped many applications and scenarios in our daily life. The Internet of Things (IoT), cloud computing, smart phones and systems are few examples of these technologies. The IoT is the technology that will enable many tools, instruments, machines, equipment to communicate with the Internet for the

H. M. Fardoun et al. (Eds.): REHAB 2016, CCIS 1002, pp. 84–97, 2019.
https://doi.org/10.1007/978-3-030-16785-1_7

purpose of sending information or receiving and executing certain commands. Cloud computing is another emerging technology [1] that facilitates the process of data storing, processing, and manipulation while reducing the complexity and cost at the end devices, thus providing a set of scalable, reliable and affordable services and applications that can be easily executed by smartphones and devices that have low cost and specifications. These evolving technologies have reformed people life in many aspects, before that, no one imagined that controlling house appliances, manufacture machines and equipment, farm irrigation systems etc., can be achieved by simply launching a mobile application especially designed to achieve these functionalities. Further, remote monitoring and sensing, where different vital parameters and symptoms can be measured, logged and sent for further processing has been greatly benefited from these technologies, which in turn improved the performance of many applications, reduced the operational cost, and speeded up the decision making process [2, 3].

Electronic healthcare services named sometimes as e-health systems are expected to be totally revolutionized utilizing these technologies. This is due to the fact that current systems that are used to monitor and log the patients' health situation are neither capable to cope-up with these new technologies nor had the needed software and hardware capabilities to be fully automated and connected to the Internet. Electronic Health Record (EHR) system is one of these important services that both the patients and doctors are anxiously looking forward, although EHR services are available in some counties [4], but many countries still lack the needed technologies for delivering these services. Another important application is remote health monitoring, which has paramount importance especially for elderly people, who may have emergency cases that need an immediate assistant. For example, an IoT based system can be used by elderly people to detect an unpredicted fall and send an alert message asking for an immediate help. To address these challenges, many companies provided e-health solutions that can facilitate patients' health monitoring, yet these systems are not affordable and cost effective to many people.

In this book chapter, we provide a more detailed description of our previous work [5] where a simple, cost effective IoT based healthcare monitoring and logging system that utilizes cloud computing is proposed, where the systems design and main components in terms of hardware and software are described in details. Further, the software code used in programing the IoT devices and the cloud network are offered to the public domain as an open source project, which will facilitate its adoption and widespread implementation thus driving people toward adopting and utilizing EHR monitoring systems, which will simplify the healthcare monitoring process, and assisting the physicians in providing the most effective medications and healthcare service to their patients. Furthermore, a fall detection system that can detect an unpredictable fall, and send an alert message to the remote healthcare personnel asking for an immediate human intervention is proposed. However, in order to improve the system efficiency and reduce the false alarms, a voice controlled system that utilizes voice recognition is proposed that will be launched once a fall incident is detected, this system will open a dialogue with the patient in order to verify whether it was a real fall that needs an assistant or it just a normal movement or false alarm that do not require an immediate help. The proposed healthcare monitoring system is based on an Arduino microcontroller [6] equipped with a set of medical sensors. The sensors measure the patients' health conditions and send them through a microcontroller to a cloud platform to form permanent medical records for the patients, which can be easily accessible by patients and doctors. The fall detection system consists of a w wearable device that utilizes an Arduino microcontroller, gyroscope and accelerometer sensor, and voice recognition module, that can detect a fall and conduct a voice verification process to check whether the patient needs an assistant or not.

The contribution of the book chapter is two folds; first, the hardware components used in the proposed system is inexpensive and affordable, further, the developed code of the proposed system is provided to the public as an open source project, which will facilitate its adoption. Second, the proposed fall detection system with the voice recognition interaction functionality is relatively new. The rest of the book chapter is organized as follows: Sect. 2 provides a brief literature review for the most related papers. Section 3 describes the proposed e-health monitoring system and its implementation. Section 4 describes the proposed fall detection system. Section 5 summarizes the paper and proposes future work.

2   Literature Review

The idea of developing an IoT health monitoring system by itself is not novel, however, very few systems are made available to the public as open source projects, and proposed cost effective solutions, which may limit the ability of deployment and adoption. Furthermore, in the literature, there are several fall detection systems and algorithms, but they just detect the fall and do not interact with the patients to confirm the fall, which may result in false alarms. The authors in [7] developed a system for ambulatory use that collects and measures the patients' health conditions using a set of wireless sensors. The collected data is stored in a local database that is sent to the physician server for further analysis and processing. Furthermore, an alarming signal is sent to both patients and doctors if any abnormal health condition is detected.

Mukherjee et al. [8] developed an e-health system that can, in real-time, monitor the patients' health conditions through a set of sensors available at the patients' premises, which in turn sends the captured data to a remote server using a smartphone or communication device for further processing and analysis, where an alert message is sent to the medical doctors in case an emergency is detected. E-health monitoring systems can also include extra features and applications like patients' fall detection. The authors in [2, 3] proposed a System of systems network architecture that can be used to provide remote health monitoring for patients, who can be residing at their homes or at the hospital, and using medical IoT sensors that are connected to the remote medical center.

Falls affect millions of people every year and could cause injuries especially for the elderly [9]. In fact, falls have been considered one of the top three causes of death in elderly people. In the literature, several algorithms and systems have been proposed in the field of elderly fall detection. In [9], Rajasekaran et al. developed a system composed of a network of wearable sensors and general computing capabilities for the individual event detection, alerts, and communications with various medical informatics services. The system purpose is to provide monitoring services for elderly patients under drug therapy after infarction, data collection in some cases, and remote consultation for elderly people. Moreover, Alazrai et al. [10, 11] proposed two approaches for fall detection, one is based on depth-map video sequences based on view-invariant human activity representation [10], while the other one detects fall using anatomical-plane-based representation [11].

There are currently some fall detection systems available that detect these falls and allow the user to obtain an assistance manually or automatically if a fall occurs. Exemplary fall detection systems can consist of personal help buttons (PHBs) or environment-based and automatic detection systems and wearable sensors. For instant, Peng et al. [12] developed a fall detection system that can detect and expect a fall after analyzing the data captured by a sensor designed for that purpose. Then the fall detector system uses the captured data to adapt and fine-tune the fall detection process according to the patient physical characteristics. Commercially, many companies started providing fall detection devices as on the shelf products; for instance, AutoAlert is a sample product from Philips company, which combines accelerometers and barometric sensors with a tuned algorithm to detect many types of falls with a claimed accuracy of 95% [13]. Apple watch series 4 offers an application that detects hard fall and connect the user to the emergency with touch screen interface [14]. Khan and Hoey concluded in their review of fall detection techniques that fall detection researcher collected their data in special settings that may be not applicable in all daily life situations and environments, which limits the accuracy of the different algorithms and techniques available and reduces the performance of classifiers significantly when the dataset used in classification is different from the training data [15]. Based on that, we believe a good fall detection system needs a further assessment technique like voice orders form the user confirming the situation.

In this work, an inexpensive and open source health monitoring system is proposed, that can be used to generate an e-health record that can be used to monitor the patient health situation, the system can also be used to analyze the logged information and detect any abnormal conditions. Furthermore, we proposed a simple yet efficient fall detection system that utilizes our previous knowledge and experience in voice recognition and dialogue systems [16, 17] is proposed, up to our knowledge there is no other system proposed in the literature that combines the detection of unpredicted fall with voice recognition, such that the system verifies whether the patient needs an assistant or not utilizing a voice recognition dialogue system, which in turn reduces the possibility of sending false alarms and improves the system accuracy.

3   E-health Monitoring System Design and Implementation

In the following sections, the design and implantation details of the proposed e-health monitoring system is provided. As depicted in Fig. 1, the e-health monitoring system consists of four main parts: a set of medical sensors, microcontroller, cloud infrastructure and web-based interface.

3.1   Medical Sensors

In order to select the most vital medical sensors, a research has been conducted in exploring the most important vital signs for medical emergencies. According to John Hopkins hospital in the US [18], vital signs are measurements of the body's most basic functions. Four main vital signs are identified and are normally monitored by medical doctors. They are the body temperature, heart pulse rate, respiration rate (rate of breathing) and blood pressure. Furthermore, in order to cover as much as possible of various health conditions, more sensors than the previously mentioned can be easily integrated into the proposed system. In particular, Electroencephalography (EEG) to measure the muscles activity, Electrocardiography (ECG) to record and monitor the heartbeat, Glucometer (blood sugar level meter) and oxygen level in the blood, patient posture and position which can be used to identify anomalous body movements and their connections with some diseases, sweating rate, and finally, the heart electrical activity (Fig. 2).

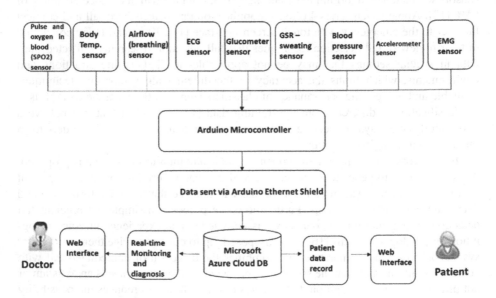

Fig. 1.   E-health monitoring system architecture

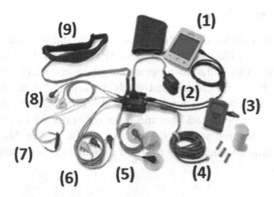

Fig. 2. The various medical sensors that can be used in this platform all connected to the e-health sensors shield. The figure depicts the following sensors: (1) Blood pressure sensor, (2) Oxygen in blood sensor, (3) Glucometer sensor, (4) Body temperature sensor, (5) Electro-cardiogram sensor, (6) Electromyography sensor, (7) Airflow sensor, (8) Galvanic skin response sensor, (9) Patient position sensor [19].

3.2 Sensors' Microcontroller Compliance

In order to build the proposed system, it was essential to find a set of sensors that are compatible with the utilized microcontroller and at the same time, cost effective and easy to integrate and deal with. This way, the proposed solution can be adopted by many people. Arduino microcontroller is an open source, cost effective, and easy to use microcontroller that was adopted in this work. Further, we tried to search for a company that provides medical sensors compatible with Arduino microcontroller. Our search leads us to a company that is specialized in electronic kits, among of them the e-health kit utilized in the proposed system [19] developed by Libelium Inc. This company not only provides the user with the sensors and the Arduino interfacing circuit, but also the software libraries and Integrated Development Environment (IDE) needed to read the sensors' data. We used these software utilities in building the Arduino code needed to interface with the sensors and to upload the sensed data to the cloud. The developed code as well as the one provided by the company [19] are made publicly available as an open source project via the Github portal [20].

3.3 Arduino Ethernet Shield

In order to send the medical sensors' data to the cloud, it is essential to equip the Arduino microcontroller with a proper communication module. In this implementation, an Ethernet shield that can be mounted on top of the microcontroller is used, which in turn provides Internet connectivity to the cloud. The main chip of this shield is the Wiznet W5100, which provides a network (IP) stack that can establish both TCP and UDP connections [21].

3.4 Microsoft Azure Cloud

Azure is Microsoft's cloud computing platform and infrastructure utilized in this project. It provides both Platform as a Service (PaaS), and Infrastructure as a Service (IaaS) and supports many different programming languages and frameworks [22]. In this project, a database was created that holds the sensors' data, which contains ten tables. The main table (user access) contains the user information, i.e. Username, password as well as the e-mail address and other user information, the remaining nine tables correspond to the nine medical sensors that can be used in this platform. Each of them contains the sensor value, the user ID and a counter to give a sequential number to the entered values.

3.5 E-health Web Interface

The system usability, privacy and security of the patients' data including his/her medical records is of utmost importance. Further, a secure access is needed to be provisioned to specific doctor to monitor and check the patients' data; hence, a web based interface portal has been developed that provides both the doctors and patients with an organized easy to use web interface for the patients' medical records.

3.6 Software Implementation Details

The aim of this section is to provide more insights into the system software implementation. In particular, the pseudocodes for capturing the sensors reading, connecting with the cloud and database schema used to save the patients' sensors information are fully described. Figure 3 depicts the pseudocode used to read the sensors readings. In line 1, the sensors are initialized by checking their statuses and by initializing specialized variables needed to store the sensors readings. Line 2 defines the buffer used to store the sensors' data. Lines 3 to 5 initialize some variables used in the code, mainly the variable used to save the captured sensors values (*value*), a counter (*i*) that will go through the sensors. The number of sensors are defined by the variable *numSensors* that is known and entered to the function readingSensors(). Further, the sensors' lower and upper normal values (*thresholdLowerValues*, *thresholdUpperValues*) are input to the function that define the normal range for the captured values, notice that these variables will be used to determine whether the captured data is normal or need an attention. Lines 7 to 15 will go through all the sensors, call the sensor (*i*) specific function getSensorValue(*i*) used to capture the sensors data, check if the captured value is normal or not, and in case of having a normal value, the captured data is stored in the *sensrosBuff* array which is returned by the readingSensors() function, if the captured data is abnormal, then the reading is marked for further investigation and analysis using the function markValue().

Once the patient's data is captured and stored into the variable *sensorsBuffer*, another function cloudConnectDBUpdate() is called. The pseudocode code of this function is shown in Fig. 4. The function starts by defining a status variable and initializing it to FALSE, this variable will be used to check whether the connection to the cloud was successfully established or not. Lines 2, 3 define the variables needed to

sensorsBuffer = **readingSensors** (*numSensors, thresholdLowerValues, thresholdUpperValues*)
1:    initSensor()
2:    **Define** *sensorsBuffer[]*
4:    **Initialize** *value* to 0
5:    **Initialize** *j* to *numSensors*
6:    **Initialize** *i* to *1*
7:    **while** *i < j* **do**
8:        *value* = getSensorValue(*i*)
9:    **if** *thresholdLowerValues [i] < value < thresholdUpperValues [i]*
10:        *sensorsBuffer[i] = value*
11:    **else :**
12:        markValue(*value, i*)
13:    **end if**
14:    *i = i + 1*
15:    **end while**

Fig. 3. Pseudocode used to read the sensors' readings

CloudConnectDBUpdate (*numSensors, sensorsBuffer*)
1:    **Initialize** *status* to FALSE
2:    **Initialize** *j* to *numSensors*
3:    **Initialize** *i* to *1*
4:    sendHttpRequest()
5:    *status* = connectionCheck()
6:    **if** *status* == FALSE
7:        display message "connection failed"
8:    **else:**
9:        **while** *i < j* **do**
10:            updateTable (*i, sensorsBuffer[i]*)
11:            *i = I +1*
12:        **end while**
13:    **end if**
14:    terminateConnection()

Fig. 4. Pseudocode used to connect to the cloud and update the database

go through the sensors. Line 4 is used to establish the connection with the MS Azure cloud platform, send an HTTP POST request to the MS Azure Mobile Service data API, and check whether the system is connected successfully to the MS Azure and the database or not, if connected, it will update the tables corresponding to the medical sensors reading stored in the *sensorsBuffer* variable using the updateTable() function.

Then the connection is terminated using the terminateConnection() function. Notice that the MS Azure cloud platform provides a time/date stamps for all the recorded data, which is very useful for monitoring the patients' health conditions over a certain period.

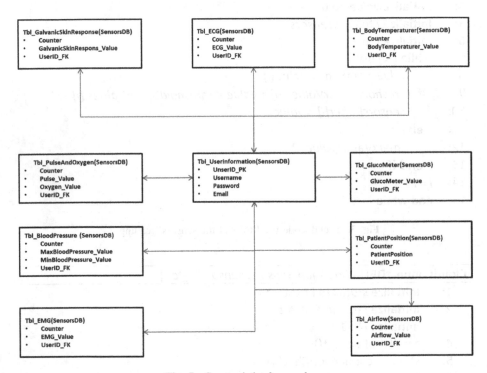

Fig. 5. Sensors' database schema

Finally, Fig. 5 depicts the database schema used to store the sensors values (SensorsDB). The database consists of several tables; the main table is the UserInformationTable, which creates a record for the patient by saving the patient basic information needed to give an access to the system and to view the records. In particular, this table saves the patient's username/password and email address. The systems also generates and saves a unique ID that is used as the database primary and foreign key. Notice that this table does not hold any private information such as the name, age, address, mobile number in order to protect the patient privacy. Further, this table is connected with the other tables that are used to hold the patient sensors' values. Notice that on each table, there is a counter field, which is incremented dynamically whenever a new record is inserted into the table.

4   Fall Detection System

After discussing the health monitoring and recording system, it is also important to discuss the other proposed system that is used to detect the patient unpredictable fall and send an alert message seeking for an immediate assistant. As described earlier, this system is designed to distinguish the unpredictable fall from daily life activities and movements. As shown in Fig. 6, the proposed system consists of a microcontroller connected to two main components:

1. A gyroscope for detecting the fall, which measures the acceleration and the rotational velocity of the patients' movements.
2. A voice recognition module that allows the user to confirm whether he/she is facing an emergency condition or not.

4.1   Programming the Gyroscope and the Voice Recognition Modules

The way the system determines the patient possible fall is by measuring the acceleration and the rotational velocity of the patient movements. Several experiments that simulate the patient fall have been tested to determine the threshold values, for both the

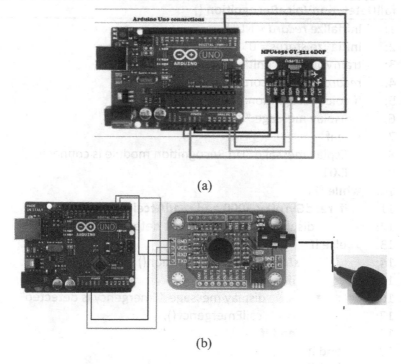

(a)

(b)

Fig. 6. Depicts the fall-detection system which consists of (a) Arduino Microcontroller connected to InvenSense MPU-6050 gyroscope and accelerometer sensor [23], and (b) Elechouse Voice Recognition Module V3 connected to the Arduino Microcontroller from the left side, and to a microphone from the right side [24]

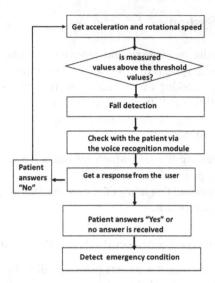

Fig. 7. A flow chart of the fall detection and emergency activation system

---

fallDetetctionVoiceRecognition ()

```
1:    Initialize record = NULL
2:    Initialize status = 0
3:    trainVoiceRecognition()
4:    record = saveRecords()
5:    if voiceRecognition.clear() == 0
6:      display message "Recognizer cleared"
7:    else if
8:      display message "No Recognition module is connected"
9:        EXIT
10:   while (1)
11:     if  readGyro() < 3000 and readAccel() < 10000
12:          display message "Fall not detected"
13:     else if
14:            status = voiceRecognition()
15:            if (status ==1)
16:                display message "Emergency is detected"
17:                callEmergency();
18:            end if
19:     end if
20:   end while
```

Fig. 8. The fall detection and voice recognition module pseudocode

acceleration and rotational velocity. When the measured values are higher than the threshold values, a fall is detected. After that, the voice activation module will start a dialogue with the patient, asking whether the patient needs an assistant or not, if the patient answers 'Yes', or if the module did not detect any comprehensible answer, then the system will assume that the patient needs an assistant and consequently activate an emergency call or send an alert message to the remote healthcare center, but in case the patient answered 'No', then the system will assume that the patient does not need any help and will not activate the automatic emergency calling process. It is worth mentioning that the automatic emergency calling and alerting process is still under further development and enhancement. Figures 7 and 8 show a flow chart of the fall detection process and the pseudocode used to program the microcontroller and the voice recognition module, respectively.

As depicted in Fig. 8, the code starts by initializing the variables (*record*, *status*) used in the voice recognition module testing, and in the fall detection, respectively. Then the recognition module is trained to match the user voice nature and characteristics using the trainVoiceRecognition() function. Lines 4 to 8 are used to check if the voice recognition module is connected properly to the microcontroller and has a valid response or not. If it is not connected, the program will exit, otherwise, it will enter in an infinite loop where it will continuously check the values of the accelerometers and Gyroscope, if they exceeded the threshold values for the normal human motion, a fall is detected and the voice recording and recognition is activated by calling the voiceRecognition() function, which will start a dialogue with the patient to check if the patient needs a help or not, if the patient answers "Yes" or provides no answer for a specific duration of time, and if the recorded message was recognized by the voice recognition module, then the system will classify this fall as a real one and will call the emergency, if the patient answers "No", then the system will consider this fall or movement as a normal one and will not call for an assistance.

5 Conclusion and Future Work

In this paper, we present our proposed e-health monitoring system which consists of a set of sensors connected to a microcontroller, where the patients' sensed vital data are uploaded to a cloud platform for recording and remote assessments. Further, we proposed a fall detection system based on a gyroscope and voice recognition module that can interact with the patient if a fall is detected. We made all the developed source code available to the public and used inexpensive and affordable off-the shelf hardware components, which should facilitate the system adoption and implementation. As a future work, we are still improving the fall detection system and the voice recognition accuracy to make it more robust against surrounding noise. Further, we are working on leveraging and integrating our previous work focused on designing a mobile application that can be used as a data mule [25] for the patient health record especially when an Internet connect may not exist. Another potential feature that can be added to the fall detection system is the one proposed in [26], which utilizes the patient position while providing healthcare monitoring service. This feature can be integrated into the proposed fall detection system, thus issuing an alert message to the closest healthcare personnel to the patient location. Working on larger dataset collected from more than one researcher to better understand and cover the unseen falls as recommended by [32] may improve the performance of the systems and algorithms. Privacy in IoT and cloud environment [27] is another important aspect that should be addressed in this proposed framework, where anonymization techniques and data hiding can be used to improve the privacy of the patients who are using this system. Moreover, we are in the process of developing an expert system that can analyze the patients' data, detect, and predict any potential health problems, so the patient will be notified automatically.

Acknowledgment. The authors would like to thank the German Jordanian University for funding this project through the Grant No. GP (13/2015).

References

1. Kiblawi, T., Khaliferh, A.: Disruptive innovations in cloud computing and their impact on business and technology. In: 2015 4th International Conference on Reliability, Infocom Technologies and Optimization (ICRITO)(Trends and Future Directions), September, pp. 1–4. IEEE (2015)
2. Khalifeh, A., Obermaisser, R., Abou-Tair, D.E.D.I., Abuteir, M.: Systems-of-systems framework for providing real-time patient monitoring and care. In: Proceedings of the 8th International Conference on Pervasive Computing Technologies for Healthcare, May, pp. 426–429. ICST (Institute for Computer Sciences, Social-Informatics and Telecommunications Engineering) (2014)
3. Obermaisser, R., Abuteir, M., Khalifeh, A., Abou-Tair, D.E.D.I.: Systems-of-systems framework for providing real-time patient monitoring and care: challenges and solutions. In: Fardoun, H.M., Penichet, V.M.R., Alghazzawi, D.M. (eds.) REHAB 2014. CCIS, vol. 515, pp. 129–142. Springer, Heidelberg (2015). https://doi.org/10.1007/978-3-662-48645-0_12
4. Ludwick, D.A., Doucette, J.: Adopting electronic medical records in primary care: lessons learned from health information systems implementation experience in seven countries. Int. J. Med. Inform. **78**(1), 22–31 (2009)
5. Khalifeh, A., Saleh, A., AL-Nuimat, M., Abou-Tair, D.E.D.I.: An open source cloud based platform for elderly health monitoring and fall detection. In: Proceedings of the 4th Workshop on ICTs for improving Patients Rehabilitation Research Techniques, October, pp. 97–100. ACM (2016)
6. Arduino microcontroller official website. http://www.arduino.cc. Accessed Oct 2018
7. Nita, L., Cretu, M., Hariton, A.: System for remote patient monitoring and data collection with applicability on e-health applications. In: 2011 7th International Symposium on Advanced Topics in Electrical Engineering (ATEE), May, pp. 1–4. IEEE (2011)
8. Mukherjee, S., Dolui, K., Datta, S.K.: Patient health management system using e-health monitoring architecture. In: 2014 IEEE International Advance Computing Conference (IACC), February, pp. 400–405. IEEE (2014)
9. Rajasekaran, M.P., Radhakrishnan, S., Subbaraj, P.: Elderly patient monitoring system using a wireless sensor network. Telemed. e-Health **15**(1), 73–79 (2009)
10. Alazrai, R., Momani, M., Daoud, M.I.: Fall detection for elderly from partially observed depth-map video sequences based on view-invariant human activity representation. Appl. Sci. **7**(4), 316 (2017)

11. Alazrai, R., Zmily, A., Mowafi, Y.: Fall detection for elderly using anatomical-plane-based representation. In: 2014 36th Annual International Conference of the IEEE Engineering in Medicine and Biology Society, August, pp. 5916–5919. IEEE (2014)
12. Peng, Y., Jin, S., Koninklijke Philips NV: Fall detection system (2013). U.S. Patent 8,381,603
13. AutoAlert: Automatic Fall Detection by Philips Lifeline. https://www.lifeline.philips.com/medical-alert-systems/fall-detection.html. Accessed Oct 2018
14. Use fall detection with Apple Watch Series 4. https://support.apple.com/en-jo/HT208944. Accessed Oct 2018
15. Khan, S.S., Hoey, J.: Review of fall detection techniques: a data availability perspective. Med. Eng. Phys. **39**, 12–22 (2017)
16. Darabkh, K.A., Khalifeh, A.F., Jafar, I.F., Bathech, B.A., Sabah, S.W.: A yet efficient communication system with hearing-impaired people based on isolated words of arabic language. IAENG Int. J. Comput. Sci. **40**(3), 183–192 (2013)
17. Khalil, R.T., Khalifeh, A., Darabkh, K.A.: Mobile-free driving with Android phones: system design and performance evaluation. In: 2012 9th International Multi-Conference on Systems, Signals and Devices (SSD), March, pp. 1–6. IEEE (2012)
18. Johns Hopkins Medical Center website. http://www.hopkinsmedicine.org/healthlibrary/conditions/cardiovascular_diseases/vital_signs_body_temperature_pulse_rate_respiration_rate_blood_pressure_85,P00866/. Accessed July 2016
19. e-health Sensor Platform V2.0 for Arduino and Raspberry Pi [Biometric/Medical Applications]. https://www.cooking-hacks.com/documentation/tutorials/ehe. Accessed July 2016
20. Github website. https://github.com/EhealthPlatform. Accessed July 2016
21. Arduino Ethernet Shield. https://www.arduino.cc/en/Main/ArduinoEthernetShield. Accessed July 2016
22. Microsoft Azure Cloud. http://azure.microsoft.com/en-us/overview/what-is-azure/. Accessed July 2016
23. MPU-6050 Accelerometer and Gyro. http://playground.arduino.cc/Main/MPU-6050. Accessed July 2016
24. Voice Recognition Module V3. http://www.elechouse.com/elechouse/images/product/VR3/VR3_manual.pdf. Accessed July 2016
25. Al-Tamimi, A.K., Khalifeh, A.: Mobile mules: modular e-health information synchronization framework. In: 2014 8th International Symposium on Medical Information and Communication Technology (ISMICT), April, pp. 1–5. IEEE (2014)
26. Hababeh, I., Alouneh, S., Khalifeh, A.F.: A position aware mobile application for e-health services. In: 2016 7th International Conference on Intelligent Systems, Modelling and Simulation (ISMS), January, pp. 144–148. IEEE (2016)
27. Abou-Tair, D.E.D.I, Büchsenstein, S., Khalifeh, A.: A privacy preserving framework for the internet of things. In: 2018 19th IEEE/ACIS International Conference on Software Engineering, Artificial Intelligence, Networking and Parallel/Distributed Computing (SNPD), June, pp. 27–31. IEEE (2018)

Serious Games for the Rehabilitation of Disabled People: Results of a Multilingual Survey

Marion Hersh[1](✉) and Barbara Leporini[2]

[1] Biomedical Engineering, University of Glasgow, Glasgow G12 8LT, Scotland
marion.hersh@glsgow.ac.uk
[2] ISTI – CNR, Via G. Moruzzi, 1, 56124 Pisa, Italy
barbara.leporini@isti.cnr.it

Abstract. The paper reports the results of an original mixed-methods survey on the experiences and attitudes of disabled people to digital games in rehabilitation. Serious games are very widely used, but there is currently no research from the perspective of disabled people on their use in rehabilitation. A majority of participants were found to consider games in rehabilitation useful or very useful, with particular interest in games with a camera and sensors. Some statistically significant differences were found between the experiences and attitudes of blind and other disabled people and under and over 40s, but the results were found to be male-female gender independent. Several theories of technology use were applied to interpret the findings. The results were used to provide recommendations for the development and implementation of serious games in rehabilitation and suggestions for further work.

Keywords: Serious games · Accessible games · Disabled people ·
Older people · Rehabilitation · Human-centred design

1 Introduction

Serious games are widely used in many different applications, including education and training. However, there has been limited research on serious games for disabled and older people, despite their potential and the popularity of digital games with players over 50, who range from 14% of the total in Germany to 29% in the USA [38]. For instance, surveys on game accessibility [40] have focused on entertainment rather than serious games, with the difference understood as serious games not having entertainment as their main purpose.

The term disabled people will be used within the framework of the social model of disability as resulting from social, environmental and attitudinal barriers. However, rehabilitation has normally been understood within a medical model framework as improving or 'restoring' function to be closer to that of a non-disabled person. Improving skills and abilities is always valuable. For instance, after a stroke most people will want to improve their speech and control and range of movement. However, there is need for a definition aligned with the social model of disability, which

H. M. Fardoun et al. (Eds.): REHAB 2016, CCIS 1002, pp. 98–115, 2019.
https://doi.org/10.1007/978-3-030-16785-1_8

includes, but is not restricted to improving skills and abilities. One approach involves examination and making paralles with the literature on independence and disability which rejects definitions of independence in terms of the ability to carry out basic tasks, as this leads to many disabled people being treated as dependent.

Alternatively, independence can be understand in terms of autonomy and self-determination. Self-determination is about having agency in one's life and being able to take action to maintain or improve its quality [37] and involves making choices and decisions, setting and attaining goals, solving problems, and self-awareness, advocacy and efficacy [39]. Autonomy is about being self-governing and having control of life and choosing how to live it [6]. This then allows rehabilitation to be defined as training of disabled or older people or following an accident or illness with the aim of increasing independence understood as autonomy and self-determination.

Both competitive and cooperative games have been found to increase motivation [4]. Serious games can also engage attention, reduce boredom in repetitive activities by providing appropriate challenge, adapt to motor skills, provide meaningful tasks and appropriate feedback, and possibly distract attention from pain, [17, 30, 32]. This makes them potentially very useful in repetitive rehabilitation activities, for instance to improve physical condition after a stroke [1]. Motion capture systems can support game-based rehabilitation by obtaining data which is fed back to the user to support relearning correct movement patterns [32]. However, the privacy management issues raised by data collection have not been discussed. Mini games lasting a few minutes can provide relatively low cost development approaches for games generally covering a specific exercise [28]. There is some evidence that games can help to promote higher order thinking and soft and social skills [13] and entertainment games can improve attention and visual perception [4]. This could be helpful in both skills training and the wider aspects of rehabilitation that go beyond it. Games involving virtual reality systems e.g. [11, 33] have considerable potential to provide interesting story lines and options for practising a range of skills in a safe environment.

Accessibility relates to the environmental characteristics of the system input and output which enable particular (groups of) users to access and use all the facilities of the system [16]. Game accessibility has been improved by using user profiles to customise the user interface, alternatives to visual feedback for blind people [18] and alternatives to auditory feedback for deaf people. These alternatives need to cover any special effects to ensure that the game does not become less interesting.

There are advantages in a design for all approach [10, 12] to make games playable and enjoyable for as diverse a population as possible. However, games have generally been aimed at disabled people with a particular impairment, frequently physical, and a design for all approach rarely used [40]. This includes several games for post-stroke rehabilitation, generally to improve arm movements [7, 8, 26, 31]. Studies show that both non-disabled and post-stroke participants generally enjoy them [7] and challenge is provided by varying the pace and associated difficulty [31]. However, they have minimal storyline or fantasy and create interest through the use of audio and visual feedback. The Wii gaming control, which requires players to use movements to play games, has been used in operational therapy with positive responses from clients and therapists [19].

A few games, including puzzle games, interaction with an intelligent agent and movement games, have been developed to support social skills development or improve attention and coordination of autistic children [2, 3, 29]. Rehabilitation games have been developed to improve the cognitive skills of children and adults with cognitive impairments [11, 14, 23, 34]. In one case, an accessible interface in a game for children with cognitive impairments involved square tiles with force resistive sensors that they step on to initiate the games [14]. Several games e.g. [9] have been developed to support people with intellectual disabilities learning to use public transport. There are a few smart phone games to teach blind children, but not adults, Braille [27]. They include games for identifying and writing Braille symbols and a 'hangman' type word identification game. An interactive game to teach Deaf children American Sign Language [5, 20, 25] includes a child signing short phrases to an on-screen cat avatar. Serious games have also been used to improve balance, provide therapeutic support for eating problems, gambling and other behavioural issues [30], as well as in the rehabilitation of people with various health conditions [22, 38].

Thus, there is a small body of work on rehabilitation games. However, most of the literature focuses on specific games and does not investigate wider issues of game design, design for all approaches and what disabled people want from them. It also generally considers rehabilitation solely in terms of improving skills and functioning and not in terms of improving independence, as defined here. This chapter aims to meet some of these gaps. In particular its aims are (i) investigating the attitudes to, knowledge of and experiences of disabled people of the use of digital and interactive games in the rehabilitation of disabled people and (ii) obtaining suggestions for improving game design and use. It will do this in a framework of the social model definition of rehabilitation presented above, an understanding of disabled people as experts on their own experiences, design for all principles and technology use theories. The technology acceptance model (TAM) [36], according to which usefulness and ease of use are the main drivers of technology use is one of the most commonly used technology use theories Other relevant theories are based on motivation with the four components of attention gaining, relevance, confidence building and satisfaction [35] and the impact of the context and structures [15]. With regard to context the availability or lack of support could be an important factor [21].

2 Methods

The study involved a questionnaire for disabled people and parents of disabled people under 16 to complete on their behalf. It has three sections. Section A covers personal information on gender, age and impairment. Section B investigates the frequency and type of use of information technology, digital games and apps. Section C investigates the use of games in rehabilitation, views on their usefulness for different age groups, activities that could be supported and comments and suggestions.

English and Italian versions were produced and care taken to ensure their equivalence. Both authors speak both languages. The questionnaire could be completed anonymously online or as a word file. The online questionnaire site was chosen to be accessible and have a good privacy policy. The links to the online version of the questionnaire were circulated to organisations of disabled people, through email lists and forums, to the authors' contacts and by other researchers and disabled people. The Fisher exact test with software developed by Langsrud [24] was used to determine statistical significance at the 0.05 level.

3 Results

Percentages are given to the nearest integer and may not add to 100% due to rounding. 44 responses were obtained, 43 from disabled people with 23 Italian and 20 English speaking and one from an English speaking parent of a disabled child under 16. 45% were female, 45% male, 2% other (and 7% unstated). There was a good age distribution, with 25% between 41 and 50 and 14–20% in each of the other decades between 20 and 70. 59%, including all the Italian participants, were blind or partially sighted, a third physically disabled, 9% deaf or hard of hearing and 5% autistic. 14% had mental health conditions, 5% specific learning difficulties, 2% general learning difficulties and 2% sensory processing difficulties. Some participants had more than one impairment.

3.1 Use of Computers and Tablets/Smartphones

All the participants used computers and 98% a smartphone or tablet. The overwhelming majority spent between 1–3 and over eight hours a day using both computers and smartphones/tablets (both 89%) (Table 1). Considerably, but not statistically significantly more of them (23% compared to 12%, p = 0.18) used computers for over eight hours a day and smartphones/tablets for 1–3 h a day (48% compared to 30%, p = 0.26). Thus, computers are still the most frequently used device, but tablets/smartphones are catching up.

The most popular applications were internet and email (Table 2), with nearly universal use of both on computers (98%) and 71% and 81% respectively on tablets/smartphones with the differences statistically significant (p = 0.0007 and 0.0009). Computers were used considerably, but not statistically significantly more often for both work (56% cf. 36%, p = 0.08) and formal education (26% cf. 17%, p = 0.4) than smartphones/tablets. Other frequent uses of computers were producing documents (77%) and finance and budgeting (35%) and of smartphones/tablets phone calls (88%) and travel (63%) and other (33%) apps. Participants mainly used digital games for entertainment (53%), followed by personal learning (37%), professional training (19%) and rehabilitation (14%), with only 7% using them in formal education. Other uses provided in the comments included with children in an educational setting, fitness, coordination, 'brain training to improve memory' and 'mental distraction'.

Table 1. Frequency of use of computers and smartphones/tablets

	Never	Very occasionally	Once a month	2–3x/week	<1 h/day	1–3 h/day	4–8 h/day	>8 h/day
Computer	0	0	2%	2%	7%	30%	36%	23%
Phone or tablet	2%	2%	0	0	7%	48%	30%	11%

Table 2. Use of computers and smartphones/tablets

	Internet	Email	Producing documents	Work	Games	Finance	Formal education	Phone calls	Travel apps	Other apps
Computer	98%	98%	77%	57%	39%	34%	25%			
Phone or tablet	70%	80%		34%	36%		16%	86%	64%	32%
Stat sig p	0.0007	0.01		.053			0.43			

3.2 Uses of Digital Games

55% (31) provided their uses of games on computers and/or tablets/smartphones, so the additional 11 presumably used games on another device than a computer or tablet/smart phone. The main application was enjoyment (77% of 31), followed by personal learning (52%), professional training (26%) and rehabilitation (19%) (Table 3). Suggested additional uses of games related to improving mental and physical functioning, specifically 'fitness and brain training to improve memory' and 'mental distraction and coordination'. 16 participants commented on their use of games. They named types of games, including puzzle, brain training and word games and specific games, including solitaire, sudoko, pokemon go, scrabble bridge and bingo rather than discussing their use.

Table 3. Types of uses of games

Use	Enjoyment	Professional training	University courses	College	School	Personal learning	Rehabilitation
%	77	26	6	0	6	52	19

13 participants commented on their use of digital games in rehabilitation, with three others commenting they did not use them. Presumably seven participants used digital games in rehabilitation on other devices than computers and smart phones/tablets. They were used for a mixture of physical and mental rehabilitation and relaxation, with several participants mentioning memory. Other applications included coordination, fitness, occupational therapy and problem solving. Approaches to improving memory included 'using the games before I go to sleep helps the following day, since playing the word games I have improved my memory which helps me talk and not 'lose' words quite as much'; and 'I use word games to try to keep my vocabulary'. Luminosity was

used multifunctionally to 'track my performance in memory, coordination, concentration to track my progress against tiredness (sleep), MS relapses and stress'. Comments about physical rehabilitation included 'Timmoco is a game that enables my kid to move his hands in order to gain some precision in his movements' and 'I use Fitbit to track how far I can walk and my sleep patterns with regard to pain'. Comments on games for relaxation included 'I play solitaire because I don't have to think about anything ... I don't even have to concentrate and I don't care what my score is.'

The main negative comment was from a participant using games 'to improve my memory and problem solving' following a therapist's recommendation. They 'prefer a book or person ... Find them hard to do ... get easily bored if I don't progress and forget to do them', indicating that games are not a universal solution. Four participants commented positively on other uses, including learning languages, entertainment and 'pass[ing] the time'. One participant deplored the lack of 'digital ... games that kids with quadriplegia can play. 'We are in need for more games that are switch or eye gaze friendly'.

3.3 The Usefulness of Games in Rehabilitation

Nearly 60% considered digital games useful (41%) or very useful (16%) in rehabilitating someone with similar impairments (Table 4). A camera or sensors that could track movements considerably increased game usefulness in rehabilitation to 80%, though the difference narrowly missed statistical significance (p = 0.08). However, this raises privacy management issues.

Table 4. Usefulness of digital games in rehabilitation

	Not at all useful	Not useful	Neither useful nor not useful	Useful	Very useful	No response
Games	0%	20%	20%	41%	16%	2%
Games with camera and sensors	0%	9%	11%	64%	16%	0%

35 participants (80%) commented on game usefulness. Several of them commented that they did not 'know of any games that could be helpful in my rehabilitation', though some of them considered 'if there are games for rehabilitation, ... then they might be useful. I would be curious.' There were also positive comments on motivation and making learning easier: 'a motivational tool for rehabilitation and entertainment for kids at the same time' and 'Could provide opportunities to support rehabilitation in ways that are engaging and/or enjoyable'; However, the importance of an appropriate degree of challenge was noted: 'If the targets are too hard I would not do it. If it becomes tiresome I would not do it. ... a small challenge'. On the negative side 'they require too much concentration for my mental health problems'.

Digital games were considered useful for learning or improving skills, including 'identifying sounds for mobility training', motor skills and sign language and 'the option of doing exercises at home', though one participant did 'not see why games would help with mobility'. There was a fun aspect, including 'collaborative enjoyment', as well as improving 'well-being' and 'state of mind'. Participants also noted games were currently little used in rehabilitation and the need for accessible games. Negative comments included preference for rehabilitation 'in person with a real person' and that games would be used to make up for the lack of therapists. 'I feel they are being used because therapists of all sorts can't see patients quick enough or as often as they would like.'

At least 32% of participants considered digital games suitable for the rehabilitation of people of all ages from preschool to over 70. The largest numbers considered them suitable for the rehabilitation of 18–30 year olds (74%), 6–12 year olds (72%) and teenagers (65%) (Table 5).

Table 5. Ages rehabilitation games considered suitable for

Age	Preschool	6–12 years	Teenagers	18–30 years	31–70 years	70+ years
%	39	73	66	75	52	32

35 participants (80%) commented on the ages games were suitable for, though several of these comments purely noted their inability to comment. The comments mainly divided into two groups, those who thought games suitable or potentially 'fun, educational and self directed' for all ages' and those who considered them better adapted to younger people. The first category included 'Everyone can get something from them' and 'There are word games that can help all ages from co-ordination for preschool to crossword type and word search games for the over 70's'. They also rejected the idea that technology could act as a barrier: 'while older people may not be as familiar with technology they could be shown', One participant specifically mentioned the benefits to an older relative: 'My Mother finds digital games entertaining at 89'.

Several comments in the second category related to younger people's greater perceived ability and liking for technology: 'I think younger people would prefer to use them or anyone who is really into phones and computer games' and 'Younger people understand the tech better and are usually more dexterous'. There was also a belief that learning was age dependent: 'probably the greatest level of learning takes place at a young age … I find it difficult to imagine game which old people can easily use'. Other comments related to school integration: 'at primary school age it could also support integration with non-disabled peers'; and sensory compensation: 'in the first years of life games could be useful to compensate for missing senses or develop residuals.'

3.4   Games with a Camera and Sensors

28 participants (64%) proposed a wide range of activities that they considered could be usefully practiced or carried out with the help of games with a camera and sensors to detect movement. One participant stated that 'the limits are determined by your imagination'. Participants were generally interested in rehabilitation related to their specific impairments. The blind participants were particularly interested in mobility, including tele-guidance via a camera and learning about the environment. Several Italian blind participants were interested in learning foreign languages, sports and dancing. The other disabled participants were interested in movement, including reaching, grabbing, coordination, walking and physiotherapy, and also mentioned sign language and sound identification.

Several comments on the usefulness of games with cameras and sensors related specifically to the value of cameras e.g. 'a game with a camera could be very useful'. Others were about rehabilitation but not specifically games e.g. 'I think a camera is fundamental, as only this way can you know whether you are doing the exercise correctly'. Practical suggestions for the use of a camera included 'to use a camera to remind people of what an item is called ... it can be very frustrating not ... to find the word to describe something'. One blind participant considered a camera more useful for people with other impairments, though 'with a distance connection to a sighted person it could help a blind person find something in the house'.

Concern was expressed about sensor sensitivity: 'they would need to accommodate individuals with impairments which means ... their movement ability, is restricted. Therefore sensors would need to be sensitive enough to detect subtle movements'. Other comments related to making games accessible to more people. 'It would enable people who lack the dexterity ... to participate in online gaming.' Other positive comments involved improving the abilities to walk in a straight line and identify sounds and use with existing equipment: 'I use adaptive equipment that reads the screen. To add a form of movement detection would be a great feature'. Several participants considered that usefulness depended on the type of game, or the user and their impairment(s). Other participants considered that they were not particularly relevant to them; and one participant was sceptical about their usefulness in mobility other than for encouraging exercise.

3.5   Reasons for Not Using Games, Types of Output and Suggestions

While most participants were relatively positive about serious digital games, including their use in rehabilitation, a significant minority (27%) did not like games (Table 6). The main reasons for not using games in rehabilitation were not knowing they were available (43%) and not participating in rehabilitation (39%) and being unaware of suitable games (39%). Lack of accessibility was an issue for a fifth and 16% considered them not useful. Several participants provided more than one reason.

Table 6. Reasons for not using games in rehabilitation

Reason	Not like games	Not participated in rehab	Not know games used in rehab	Unaware of suitable games	Not consider useful	Digital games not accessible	Other
%	27	39	43	39	16	20	7

Overall participants considered sounds the most useful output from a digital game (4.4 out of 5), followed by speech (3.5) and vibration (3.4) with pressure or tapping (2.5) and other tactile indications (2.7) considered the least useful (Table 7). Most of the differences were statistically significant e.g. $p = 0.0001$ for sound and speech and $p = 0.001$ for speech and pressure or tapping. Statistically significant differences between blind and other disabled people included other disabled people considering pressure or tapping (3.6 cf 2.1) and other tactile input (3.2 cf. 2.1) more useful than blind people and vibration less useful (2.4 cf. 4.2). The differences between under and over 40s were small.

Table 7. Attitudes to different types of output

	Vibration	Press/tapping	Other tactile	Speech	Sounds
Overall (%)	3.7	2.7	2.5	3.8	4.4
Blind (%)	4.2	2.1	2.1	3.4	4.6
Other disabled	2.4	3.6	3.2	3.9	4.1
P	10^{-7}	0.00003	0.004		

29 participants (66%) commented on the use of sources of information other than sounds, speech, vibration, tapping/pressure or other tactile. A blind participant commented that 'any type of information could be useful'. Other comments by blind people suggested a combination of sound and vibration e.g. 'for speed of operation the combination sound-vibration is superior to speech' or a combination of sound, speech and vibration e.g. 'sound, vibration and spoken comments ... when combined ... can ... make the difference in using a game, whether for fun, education or rehabilitation'. The other disabled participants either focussed on their specific requirements or the importance of considering the needs of users with different impairments. The latter included 'different needs, different ways of information so universal design should be applied'; 'all of the above are necessary, and this includes sound, particularly for those with visual or learning difficulties.' The need for silent devices was recognised: 'for sound should not be the only criteria for entry (e.g. if disabled people require their device to be on silent)' and 'vibration is useful, as it is discrete and practical'. The need of sensory development to enjoy games was also suggested: 'The senses that are engaged using games need to be educated in order to gain any gratification'.

A parent commented on their hearing impaired son's need for visual, including sign language information: 'my son has hearing loss, in that case a sign language information or symbols, or pictures would be useful'. Participants with impairments affecting tactile perception and dexterity were unsure about the usefulness of tactile information and preferred speech. 'I have difficulties to concentrate feeling vibrations. I don't know what other tactile information can be useful' and 'As someone with very limited dexterity I would find games where I could complete actions via two word speech commands "shoot B" (for example)'. Users with sensory processing issues needed carefully managed input: 'I've got sensory processing issues ... I can tap on a screen and I can read text/look at images, but please don't talk to me or expect me to get more from auditory information than "there's a sound!" when I am playing a GAME'.

Suggestions for the use of digital games to support rehabilitation or education included the need for games with a single switch; the use of sound and vibration, for instance to learn about space, and maps and Braille labels on CD boxes. Several participants stressed the importance of making existing games for non-disabled people accessible for everyone, if appropriate with the use of assistive technology, and the need to make games usable and simple. The appropriate use of games with attention to both their advantages and disadvantages was recommended. 'Games are good for improving concentration but also as a distraction. I am not sure if they are the be all and end all to disability but I am sure they could improve situations for most people.' Suggested uses included improving memory and motor rehabilitation.

3.6 Comparisons for Gender, Age and Type of Impairment

The data was found to be male-female gender independent with similar values for frequency and type of use of both computers and tablets/smartphones, game applications, the perceived usefulness of rehabilitation games for different ages and with and without cameras and sensors. As an example usefulness of rehabilitation games is given in Table 8.

Table 8. Gender similarities in game usefulness

	M/F	Not at all useful	Not useful	Neither useful nor not useful	Useful	Very useful
Games (%)	F	0	20	10	35	30
Games (%)	M	0	20	10	35	25

The main differences in the responses of blind and other disabled participants, and participants over and under 40 are discussed briefly below. Almost all participants in these four groups used computers for both internet and email. Fewer blind than other disabled participants played games on both computers (31% cf. 50%, p = 0.22) and tablets/smartphones (23% cf 56%, p = 0.054) with the latter difference close to statistical significance. The main other differences were greater use of computers for finance and budgeting and statistically significantly greater use of other apps on tablets/smartphones by other disabled than blind people (50% cf. 19%, p = 0.049). More under 40s used computers in formal education and over 40s for finance and budgeting, but the differences were not statistically significant, Similar numbers of over and under 40s used tablets/smartphones for education. More over 40s used other apps on tablets/smartphones and more under 40s travel apps (82% cf. 52%, p = 0.056), with the later difference close to statistical significance.

Approximately equal numbers of blind (59%) and other disabled people (56%) considered games to be useful or very useful in rehabilitation and somewhat more blind people (85% cf. 72%) considered games with sensors and cameras useful or very useful in rehabilitation. However, in both categories more blind people considered games useful and more other disabled people very useful. More under than over 40s considered games with (88% cf. 75%) and without (71% cf. 58%) a camera and sensors useful or very useful.

More blind people used games for personal learning (50% cf. 17%, p = 0.03) and professional training (23% cf. 11%, p = 0.03) and fewer for rehabilitation (8% cf. 22%), with the first two differences statistically significant. More under than over 40s used games for enjoyment (76% cf. 41%, p = 0.03) and personal learning (52% cf. 26%, p = 0.11) and fewer for rehabilitation (0 cf. 22%. p = 0.002), with the first and last differences statistically significant. The difference in use for enjoyment may be indicative of different attitudes to games.

Significantly more other disabled than blind people considered games suitable for the rehabilitation of preschoolers (61% cf to 23%, p = 0.015) and people over 71 years (61% cf. 12%, p = 0.0009). More under than over 40s considered games suitable for each age group, with the total differences (p = 0.0001) and those for teenagers (88% cf. 52%, p = 0.02) statistically significant.

More blind than other disabled people did not use games in rehabilitation, because they did not like them, had not participated in rehabilitation, did not know games were used in rehabilitation, were unaware of suitable games and found digital games inaccessible with the overall (p = 0.004), but not individual differences statistically significant. However, fewer blind than other disabled people did not consider games useful in rehabilitation, but the difference was not statistically significant. More under than over 40s did not use games in rehabilitation as they had not participated in rehabilitation (71% cf 19%, p = 0.0003) or did not know that games could be used in rehabilitation (76% cf. 22%, p = 0.0005). More under than over 40s were unaware of suitable games and considered them not useful and more over 40s did not like games, but the differences were not statistically significant. Approximately equal numbers (18% cf. 22%) of both under and over 40s considered that digital games were not accessible.

4 Discussion and Conclusions

The results of the survey show that a diverse group of disabled people are very frequent users of both computers and smartphones/tablets for a range of applications. While they currently use computers more, the relative closeness of the figures indicate that smartphones/tablets may soon take over. This increasing popularity is probably due to their easy portability and indicates that many disabled people are able to overcome the potential accessibility barriers resulting from their small size.

Over half the participants used digital games for enjoyment and just over a third for personal learning, and a significant minority (14%) already used them in rehabilitation. Over 60% of participants considered games useful in the rehabilitation of someone with similar impairments and this increased to over 80% for games with cameras and sensors to track movement. [Most people think that games in the rehabilitation can be mostly useful for young users (from 16 to 30), but only a small sample considers such a valuable support for prescholar individuals.] Thus there is a considerable gap between the percentage of participants who considered games useful in rehabilitation and those who actually used them. While just over a quarter of participants did not like digital games, the main reasons for not using games in rehabilitation, each held by about 40% of participants, were lack of knowledge of their potential and lack of knowledge of suitable games and not having participated in rehabilitation. This indicates the potential for the use of games in rehabilitation, as well as need to develop additional games. While nearly a third of participants considered digital serious games suitable for rehabilitation for all ages, nearly two thirds considered them most suitable for children, teenagers and young adults.

From the responses participants' understanding of rehabilitation seems to generally be the traditional one of improving skills and functioning rather than the wider social model understanding proposed here. Thus participants considered games to be useful in mobility training, motor skills, sign language and exercising at home, and games with a camera to remind people of object names. The expressed interest in games for learning languages could be related to the social model understanding of rehabilitation or indicate a misunderstanding of the concept.

There were some interesting differences and similarities between the different groups of participants. In particular, the results on device frequency, games applications and the perceived usefulness of rehabilitation games for different ages and with and without cameras and sensors were male-female gender independent. This is interesting, as gender is generally considered to be an important variable in technology use. Participants under 40 were more aware than over 40s of the potential of digital games for rehabilitation for older age groups, indicating the need for both appropriate design and awareness raising. The main game related differences and similarities are summarised below:

- Game playing: fewer blind than other disabled played games on both tablets/ smartphones (close to statistical significance) and computers.
- Useful or very useful in rehabilitation: equal numbers of blind and other disabled people; more blind people for games with camera and sensors; more under than over 40s for games with and without sensors and camera.
- Game applications: significantly more blind people for personal learning and professional training and fewer for rehabilitation; significantly more under than over 40s for enjoyment and personal learning and significantly fewer for rehabilitation.
- Reasons games not used in rehabilitation: more blind people do not like them, not participated in rehabilitation, not know games used, not aware of suitable games and have accessibility issues (overall statistically significant); more under 40s have not participated in rehabilitation, not know games could be used (both statistically significant), unaware of suitable games and not consider them useful; more over 40s did not like games; about the same under and over 40s found games inaccessible.

While the majority of participants considered games useful, a significant minority was sceptical about the usefulness of games in rehabilitation. More over than under 40s did not consider them useful, though statistically significantly more over 40s used them in rehabilitation. In addition, fewer blind than other disabled people used them in rehabilitation.

From Table 6 of the reasons for not using games in rehabilitation, usefulness and ease of use in line with TAM [36] are clearly important factors. However, lack of usefulness is measured here more strongly by non-participation in rehabilitation than perceived non-usefulness. The lack of knowledge that games are used in rehabilitation and awareness of suitable games is in accordance with the attention gaining component of motivation theory, whereas not liking games is an element of lack of satisfaction [35]. However, TAM was not able to explain the experience of under and over 40s: the over 40s were using games more in rehabilitation, but considered them less useful. In terms of motivation [35] over 40s experienced some lack of satisfaction and relevance due to not liking games and not considering them useful, though there was reasonable 'attention' to games in terms of awareness of suitable games. The reduced serious game use by blind people, both in general and for rehabilitation is in accordance with both TAM and motivation theory. Blind people had reduced participation in rehabilitation (usefulness), though they considered games for rehabilitation equally useful, did not like games (satisfaction), and were not aware games were used or of suitable games (attention gaining).

The numerical data and comments indicate some of the factors to be taken into account in game development and lead to the following design and implementation recommendations:

1. Where feasible include cameras and sensors in games, with sensors sufficiently sensitive to track faint movements.
2. Make games accessible and easy to use.
3. Modify existing games to make them fully accessible, possibly through the use of assistive technology.
4. Apply design for all approaches whenever feasible.
5. Design games for neglected groups e.g. switch and eye gaze technology users
6. Make game design age appropriate and pay particular attention to the needs of older players.
7. Use games to complement other approaches rather than to replace therapists
8. Publicise the potential of rehabilitation games, particularly for older people.

The main limitations of the study are the relatively small sample size, though studies of disabled people are generally smaller than of non-disabled people, not asking about a wider range of output formats than those of interest to blind people and omitting question on country and ethnicity/race However, the results indicate the value of continuing the survey, possibly in additional countries, with the aim of obtaining more respondents and including this data.

Although feedback and comments are generally positive about technology use in rehabilitation, but some of the comments and opinions expressed indicate that partic-ipants may not fully understand the potential of technology to support disabled people. They may still consider games purely as a form of entertainment and not fully understand their potential in education training, including rehabilitation. Further research is required to investigate this.

Other avenues for further work include:

1. A survey on the use of games in rehabilitation from the perspective of professionals and a comparison of the experiences and attitudes of disabled people and professionals
2. An investigation of the potential of sensors of different types in providing feedback on user behaviour and enabling adaptive learning and users' preferences for games with sensors in addition to a camera.
3. An in-depth investigation of privacy management issues associated with data collection and the trade-offs users are willing to make.
4. An investigation of the impact of the context, including available support, and surrounding structures on the use of games in rehabilitation in line with the theory of structurisation [15].

In summary the study has indicated the potential of games in rehabilitation and made a number of recommendations for their design and implementation, as well as suggestions for further work. It has also shown the importance of the involvement of end-users in the process to both ensure that their requirements are met and to enable them to understand the potential of rehabilitation games.

Acknowledgements. We would like to thank everyone who completed a questionnaire or helped distribute them. We are very grateful for their assistance. Ethical Approval was obtained from the Ethics Committee of the College of Science and Engineering at the University of Glasgow. There are no conflicts of interest. An earlier version of the paper was published as Serious Games for the Rehabilitation of Disabled People in Rehab 2016 Workshop, ACM Digital Library.

Appendix 1 Section C The Use of Games for Rehabilitation

Questions 11–15 are for people who use games in rehabilitation. Question 18 is for those who do not. Questions 17–32 are for everyone.

11. What digital games do you use?
    a. In general
    b. In rehabilitation
12. What type of rehabilitation do you use these games for?
13. Please describe briefly your use of these games in rehabilitation
14. How often would use typically use digital games during a programme of rehabilitation?

    More than 4 hours a day____
    2–4 hours a day____
    Once 1 day____
    2 or 3 times a week____
    Once a week____

Once a month___
It depends___
Other please specify _____

15. Please comment on your use of digital games, particularly in rehabilitation
16. If you do not use or rarely use digital games either on computer or smart phone/table why is this? (please indicate all that hold)

I do not like games or have not found any digital games I like____
I have not participated in rehabilitation____
I did not know that games were available for rehabilitation____
I am not aware of suitable games____
I do not think that they would be useful for me____
I do not find digital games accessible____
Other please specify _____

17. Do you think that digital games could be useful to support your rehabilitation or the rehabilitation of other people with similar disabilities?

Not at all useful___
Not useful___
Neither useful nor not useful___
Useful___
Very useful___

18. Please comment on your reply to the previous question
19. For what age groups do you think digital games could be useful in rehabilitation? (please indicate all that hold)

For preschool children____
For children from 6 to 12 years____
For teenagers____
For young adults (18–30 years)____
For adults (31–70 years)____
For older people (over 70 years)____

20. Please comment on your replies to the previous question
21. Do you think that digital games with a camera or other sensors able to detect movement would be useful in your rehabilitation or that of people with similar disabilities?

Not at all useful___
Not useful___
Neither useful nor not useful___
Useful___
Very useful___

22. Please comment on your replies to the previous question.
23. What activities could you or other disabled people usefully practice or carry out with the aid of a game with sensors and cameras?
24. Please comment on your reply to the previous question.

25–30. Indicate from 1 (not at all useful) to 5 (very useful) how useful you consider X as a way for a digital game to give you information. 25 vibration; 26 pressure or tapping; 27 other tactile information; 28 speech; 29 sound; 30 other types of information.

31. Please comment on your replies to questions 25–30.

32. Please give further comments and suggestions for the use of digital games to support rehabilitation and/or education.

References

1. Alankus, G., Lazar, A., May, M., Kelleher, C.: Towards customizable games for stroke rehabilitation. In: Proceedings of the SIGCHI Conference on Human Factors in Computing Systems, New York, pp. 2113–2122 (2010)
2. Bartoli, L., Corradi, C., Garzotto, F., Valoriani, M.: Exploring motion-based touchless games for autistic children's learning. In: Proceedings of the 12th International Conference on Interaction Design and Children, pp. 102–111 (2013)
3. Bernardini, S., Porayska-Pomsta, K., Smith, T.J.: ECHOES: an intelligent serious game for fostering social communication in children with autism. Inf. Sci. **264**, 41–60 (2014)
4. Boyle, E.A., Hainey, T., Connolly, T.M., et al.: An update to the systematic literature review of empirical evidence of the impacts and outcomes of computer games and serious games. Comput. Educ. **94**, 178–192 (2016)
5. Brashear, H., Henderson, V., Park, K.H., et al.: American sign language recognition in game development for deaf children. In: Proceedings of the 8th International ACM SIGACCESS Conference on Computers and Accessibility, pp. 79–86 (2006)
6. Brisenden, S.: Independent living and the medical model of disability. Disabil. Handicap Soc. **1**(2), 173–178 (1986). https://doi.org/10.1080/02674648666780171
7. Burke, J.W., McNeill, M.D.J., Charles, D.K., et al.: Optimising engagement for stroke rehabilitation using serious games. Vis. Comput. **25**(12), 1085 (2009)
8. Burke, J.W., McNeill, M.D.J., Charles, D.K., et al.: Serious games for upper limb rehabilitation following stroke. In: Proceedings of the Conference on VS-GAMES 2009, pp. 103–110 (2009)
9. Cano, A.R., Fernández-Manjón, B., García-Tejedor, Á.J.: Using game learning analytics for validating the design of a learning game for adults with intellectual disabilities. Br. J. Edu. Technol. **49**(4), 659–672 (2018)
10. CEN: CEN workshop agreement CWA 14661. Guidelines to standardisers of ICT products and services in the CEN ICT domain (2003). ftp://cenftp1.cenorm.be/PUBLIC/CWAs/e-Europe/DFA/cwa14661-00-2003-Feb.pdf. Accessed 12 Aug 2010
11. Cherniack, E.P.: Not just fun and games: applications of virtual reality in the identification and rehabilitation of cognitive disorders of the elderly. Disabil. Rehabil.: Assist. Technol. **6**(4), 283–289 (2011)
12. Connell, B.R. et al.: The principles of universal design version 2.0 (1997). http://www.design.ncsu.edu/cud/about_ud/udprinciplestext.htm. Accessed 11 Aug 2010
13. Connolly, T.M., Boyle, E.A., MacArthur, E., et al.: A systematic literature review of empirical evidence on computer games and serious games. Comput. Educ. **59**(2), 661–686 (2012)

14. Dandashi, A., Karkar, A.G., Saad, S., et al.: Enhancing the cognitive and learning skills of children with intellectual disability through physical activity and edutainment games. Int. J. Distrib. Sens. Netw. **11**(6) (2015)
15. DeSanctis, G., Poole, M.S.: Capturing the complexity in advanced technology use: adaptive structuration theory. Organ. Sci. **5**(2), 121–147 (1994)
16. Federici, S., et al.: Checking an integrated model of web accessibility and usability evaluation for disabled people. Disabil. Rehabil. **27**(13), 781–790 (2005)
17. Flores, E., Tobon, G., Cavallaro, E., et al.: Improving patient motivation in game development for motor deficit rehabilitation. In: Proceedings of the International Conference on Advances in Computer Entertainment Technology, pp. 381–384 (2008)
18. Grammenos, D., Savidis, A., Stephanidis, C.: Designing universally accessible games. Comput. Entertain. **7**(1), Article 8 (2009)
19. Halton, J.: Virtual rehabilitation with video games: a new frontier for occupational therapy. Occup. Ther. Now **9**(6), 12–14 (2008)
20. Henderson, V., Lee, S., Brashear, H., et al.: Development of an American Sign Language game for deaf children. In: Proceedings of the Conference on Interaction Design and Children, pp. 70–79 (2005)
21. Hersh, M.A., Johnson, M.A.: On modelling assistive technology systems part I: modelling framework. Technol. Disabil. **20**(3), 193–215 (2008)
22. Kato, P.M.: Video games in health care: closing the gap. Rev. Gen. Psychol. **14**(2), 113 (2010)
23. Kueider, A.M., Parisi, J.M., Gross, A.L., et al.: Computerized cognitive training with older adults: a systematic review. PLoS One **7**(7), e40588 (2012)
24. Langsrud, Ø. http://www.langsrud.com/fisher.htm. Accessed 20 Nov 2018
25. Lee, S., Henderson, V., Hamilton, H., et al.: A gesture-based American Sign Language game for deaf children. In: Proceedings of the CHI 2005 Extended Abstracts on Human Factors in Computing Systems, pp. 1589–1592 (2005)
26. Ma, M., Bechkoum, K.: Serious games for movement therapy after stroke. In: Proceedings of the IEEE International Conference on Systems, Man and Cybernetics, pp. 1872–1877 (2008)
27. Milne, L.R., Bennett, C.L., Ladner, R.E., et al.: BraillePlay: educational smartphone games for blind children. In: Proceedings of the 16th International ACM SIGACCESS Conference on Computers and Accessibility, pp. 137–144 (2014)
28. Omelina, L., Jansen, B., Bonnechere, B., et al.: Serious games for physical rehabilitation: designing highly configurable and adaptable games. In: Proceedings of the 9th International Conference on Disability, Virtual Reality and Associated Technologies, pp. 195–201 (2012)
29. Piper, A.M., O'Brien, E., Morris, M.R., et al.: SIDES: a cooperative tabletop computer game for social skills development. In: Proceedings of the 20th Anniversary Conference on Computer Supported Cooperative Work, pp. 1–10 (2006)
30. Rego, P., Moreira, P.M., Reis, L.P.: Serious games for rehabilitation: a survey and a classification towards a taxonomy. In: Proceedings of the 5th Iberian Conference on Information Systems and Technologies, Santiago de Compostela, pp. 1–6 (2010)
31. Saini, S., Rambli, D.R.A., Sulaiman, S., et al.: A low-cost game framework for a home-based stroke rehabilitation system. In: Computer and Information Science International Conference, vol. 1, pp. 55–60 (2012)
32. Schönauer, C., Pintaric, T., Kaufmann, H.: Full body interaction for serious games in motor rehabilitation. In: Proceedings of the 2nd Augmented Human International Conference, p. 4 (2011)
33. Standen, P.J., Brown, D.J.: Virtual reality in the rehabilitation of people with intellectual disabilities. Cyberpsychology Behav. **8**(3), 272–282 (2005)

34. Standen, P.J., Rees, F., Brown, D.J.: Effect of playing computer games on decision making in people with intellectual disabilities. J. Assist. Technol. **3**(2), 4–12 (2009)
35. Surry, D.W., Land, S.M.: Strategies for motivating higher education faculty to use technology. Innov. Educ. Train. Int. **37**(2), 145–153 (2000)
36. Venkatesh, V., Davis, F.D.: A theoretical extension of the technology acceptance model: four longitudinal field studies. Manag. Sci. **46**(2), 186–204 (2000)
37. Wehmeyer, M.L.: Self-determination and individuals with severe disabilities: re-examining meanings and misinterpretations. Res. Pract. Persons Sev. Disabil. **30**(3), 113–120 (2005). https://doi.org/10.2511/rpsd.30.3.113
38. Wiemeyer, J., Kliem, A.: Serious games in prevention and rehabilitation—a new panacea for elderly people. Eur. Rev. Aging Phys. Act. **9**(1), 41–50 (2012)
39. Wood, W.M., Fowler, C.H., Uphold, N., Test, D.W.: A review of self-determination interventions with individuals with severe disabilities. Res. Pract. Persons Sev. Disabil. **30**(3), 121–146 (2005). https://doi.org/10.2511/rpsd.30.3.121
40. Yuan, B., Folmer, E., Harris Jr., F.C.: Game accessibility: a survey. Univ. Access Inf. Soc. **10**(1), 81–100 (2011)

Does Length Really Matter? Effects of Number of Pages in the Informed Consent on Reading Behavior: An Eye-Tracking Study

Pedro J. Rosa[1,2,3,5]($\boxtimes$), Paulo Lopes[1,2], Jorge Oliveira[1,2],
and Patrícia Pascoal[1,4]

[1] ECPV, Universidade Lusófona de Humanidades e Tecnologias,
Lisbon, Portugal
{pedro.rosa,paulo.lopes,jorge.oliveira,
patricia.pascoal}@ulusofona.pt
[2] HEI-Lab, Universidade Lusófona de Humanidades e Tecnologias,
Lisbon, Portugal
[3] Instituto Universitário de Lisboa (ISCTE-IUL), Cis-IUL, Lisbon, Portugal
[4] CICPSI, Faculdade de Psicologia, Universidade de Lisboa, Lisbon, Portugal
[5] School of Psychology and Life Sciences, ULHT, Lisbon, Portugal

Abstract. The use of an adequate informed consent (IC) is a current concern in psychological research. A good understanding of the IC is an important step to certify that the participant's decision to participate in research is informed and free. However, the number of pages in the IC may be a main hinder factor in both reading and understanding the IC. The length of information in ICs has been a matter of debate for a long time, however, no clear guidance has been given. As the reading process requires visual attention, eye movements can provide an objective and quantitative measure of visual behavior that can also be viewed as a proxy of reading behavior. Thus, the objective of this study was to examine how the number of pages in the IC influences reading behavior. Sixty participants were randomly assigned in three experimental conditions (1 page vs. 2 pages vs. 3 pages) while eye movements and the reading time were recorded. Results have shown no differences in average reading time between different lengths. However, a larger number of fixations per word was found at the bottom of the page (area of signature) in the IC with one page in comparison to the bottom of the page in ICs with two or three pages. These findings demonstrate that eye movements are a rich source of information by providing details of relevant/irrelevant contents in the IC.

Keywords: Informed consent · Number of pages · Reading behavior ·
Eye movements · Eye tracking

1 Introduction

Respect for human dignity requires that researchers obtain informed consent (IC) before conducting their research. However, in many situations, this process may be reduced to simply obtaining the participant's signature on the consent form [1][1].

---

[1] This chapter is an extended version of the paper published in the proceedings of the 4th Workshop on ICTs for Improving Patient Rehabilitation Research Techniques (REHAB, 2016).

© Springer Nature Switzerland AG 2019
H. M. Fardoun et al. (Eds.): REHAB 2016, CCIS 1002, pp. 116–125, 2019.
https://doi.org/10.1007/978-3-030-16785-1_9

Unfortunately, people often do not read or understand these documents, nor are they encouraged to do so [1–3]. The ethical concept of IC has now become standard practice in all help professions [4], can be defined as a legal, ethical and regulatory pre-requisite necessary to conduct research with human beings [5]. The IC refers to fully apprising participants and contains information about the purpose of the study, their rights, and responsibilities, confidentiality issues, methods, benefits and risks of the study and make sure the well-being of the participant is not compromised for the research [6, 7]. The Nuremberg Code and Helsinki's Declaration aggregate the guiding principles of ethical conduct, serving to protect the participant and to respect the participant's autonomy [8]. Therefore, the reading of the IC is a crucial step in any investigation, offering the participant the opportunity to voluntarily decide whether or not to participate in the research. The IC can be thought as a process that involves four phases: (1) presenting the IC to the subject; (2) explaining all the issues associated with the study; (3) considering whether interests are compatible with the objectives of the study, and (4) giving authorization for the study [9]. These steps of the IC are also used for obtaining permission for participants to enroll in clinical trial studies or certain medical exams or treatments that may have secondary negative effects and also to implement rehabilitation techniques [10, 11]. In this context, the IC must refer to the objectives and all the procedures used in rehabilitation, the potential risk for the patient and the benefits of treatment. This way, the patient and/or his caregiver can make an informed and safe choice about the rehabilitation or medical exam/treatment [12]. Therefore, it is important for the researcher/health specialist to ensure that IC contains only the required amount of information that does not compromise the attention and subsequently the understanding of the information presented.

In some cases, it is necessary to present the participant an IC with more detailed information, for instance, when it is about the use of medication or about a medical exam since these may involve a bigger risk for the participant [13]. Some important considerations that should be taken into account: (i) the number of pages of the IC influences the reading: the larger the size of IC, the lower the probability of the participant reading it; (ii) the IC should not contain excessive information, in order to improve understanding; (iii) there should be fewer numbers of pages to make the reading easier; (iv) use of colloquial and appropriate written language to all participants, that assure full understanding of all information, regardless of their literacy skills [12, 14, 15].

The study of reading via the measurement and analysis of eye movements is a large field of scientific endeavor [15]. As reading is dependent on selective attention, eye movement analysis can give a rich information during a meaningful and ecologically valid task [16–20]. It is relevant to understand if there are different patterns of reading when ICs with different number of pages are given to the subject. To our knowledge, only one study has been conducted to evaluate the reading behavior of an IC through eye tracking [21]. However, in this latter study eye measurements were examined via conventional repeated-measures ANOVAs which are not flexible enough to accommodate all of the special features of repeated measures' design. The objective of the present study is to deepen the understanding of the influence of the number of pages in IC on reading behavior via Generalized Estimating Equations (GEE) to produce more efficient estimates of ocular and behavioral metrics. Our hypothesis is that a smaller IC has a larger relative reading depth, therefore, slower reading, because usually readers do not get tangled up with long arguments. In the present study, we have used the reading depth measure that can be defined as the total time spent in an area of interest (AOI) per cm^2 or px^2 and is an indication of how densely an AOI is processed [22].

2   Method

2.1   Participants

The sample of this study consisted of 60 university students of the Universidade Lusófona de Humanidades e Tecnologias, in Lisbon. Of these, 73.3% ($n = 44$) were female and 26.7% ($n = 16$) were male. The mean age was 21.88 years old ($SD = 3.92$). Most participants were Portuguese (95.2%), 60% participants ($n = 36$) mentioned to have basic knowledge of computers and 50% ($n = 30$) mentioned that use occasionally digital drawing pad. Most of the participants mentioned having 12 years of literacy (55%). All participants reported normal medical history and no visual problems. The main exclusion criteria were: (i) history of psychiatric disorders or drug addiction condition. All participants were well informed about the study in accordance with APA's ethical principles of psychologists and code of conduct and signed an online version of an IC [23].

2.2   Measures

The instruments applied in this study were a digital IC, a socio-demographic questionnaire and a fatigue scale. A socio-demographic questionnaire was applied in digital format via Google forms, in which participants were asked about their literacy, age, sex, nationality, computer experience, and digital drawing pad experience. The fatigue was assessed through the Pichot fatigue scale which is a self-rating scale composed of eight items, rated in 4-point of scale ranging from "0" (not at all) to "4" (extremely). Participant's responses are summated in order to get a total score. The higher the score, the more fatigued the respondent is. This scale was also applied in a digital format [24]. The materials used were the Eye Tracker Tobii T60 and the digital drawing pad Wacom Intuos with 8.3-by-7.0 inches, (Fig. 1).

The eye tracker allowed us to record eye movements while participants were reading the IC. The digital pad was also used by participants to sign the IC. Three regions of interest (ROIs) were created for each page of the IC, that is, each page was divided into three identical parts, each ROI was one-third of the page (top of the page – ROI 1; the middle part of the page – ROI 2; and bottom of the page – ROI 3) (Fig. 2).

Fig. 1. Wacom digital drawing pad used in the present study

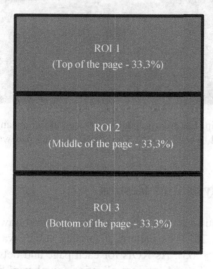

Fig. 2. Division of ROIs of each page in the IC

2.3 Procedure and Apparatus

The experiment occurred in a single session, in a soundproof laboratory room with constant illumination (42 lx). Each participant signed a consent form and was seated at the distance of 60 cm from the eye tracker (Fig. 3).

After having successfully filled out the protocol, a 9-point calibration procedure was applied. In this study, there were three between-subject conditions, consisting of ICs with different lengths (IC with 1 page vs. IC with 2 pages vs. IC with 3 pages). All conditions were balanced and randomized in order. ICs were displayed through in an Intel core2duo 6550 desktop computer, which was connected to a Tobii-T60 ET System (Tobii Technology AB, Sweden) and integrated into a 17″ TFT. Eye movements were binocularly recorded at 60 Hz, with a spatial accuracy of 0.5° of visual angle, during whole the experiment. After the task was accomplished, participants were thanked, debriefed and finally dismissed.

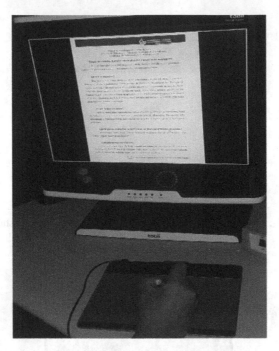

Fig. 3. Experimental setup. Each participant was seated at the distance of 60 cm from the eye tracker and was instructed to read the IC. The digital drawing pad was used for signing the IC

3 Statistical Analysis and Results

Eye blinks, drifts, and outliers (± 2 SD) were removed from raw gaze data and coded as missing values [16, 25, 26]. The pattern of missing values was completely at random (Little's MCAR test, $p > .05$). As ROIs for each page and between ICs were different in terms of the number of words, a normalization (number of fixations in ROI divided by the number of words in ROI) was applied following the guidelines provided by Holmqvist and colleagues [22]. An analysis of covariance (ANCOVA) was performed to compare the reading time between the three experimental conditions, using fatigue, computer experience and digital drawing pad experience as covariates. The ANCOVA revealed no effect of IC length on reading time, $F (2, 54) = 0.76$, $p = .474$, after the effect of covariates has been accounted for. To determine whether reading depth in the first and last pages significantly differs across experimental conditions and ROIs, GEE with identity link and normal distribution were chosen. A m-dependent working correlation matrix (m = 2) was estimated and model-based standard errors were used. This type of correlation structure was chosen as the quasi-likelihood under the independence model criterion (QIC) was the lowest [27]. Sidak correction was applied to all post-hoc tests and statistical significance was set at $p < .05$. Results have shown an interaction effect between ROI and experimental conditions, Wald $\chi^2(4) = 6.46$, $p = .019$.

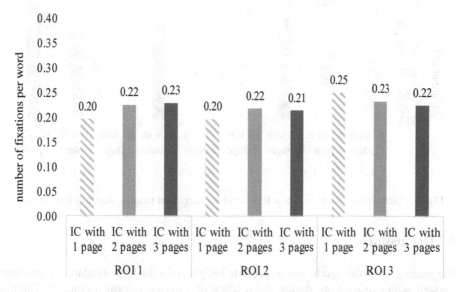

Fig. 4. Interaction effects between ROIs and IC length on reading depth in the first page

As depicted in Fig. 4, those who read the IC with one page (first experimental condition), have shown a higher number of ocular fixations per word in ROI 3 (bottom of the page) than in ROI 1 (top of the page). However, no differences were found for other ROIs. It was also compared the reading depth of the last page in each IC. In the case of the IC with one page, the first and last pages were exactly the same. The results have shown again an interaction effect between ROIs and experimental conditions, Wald $\chi^2(4) = 20.53$, $p < .001$. The multiple mean comparison revealed that participants who had read the IC with two or three pages, performed a deeper reading in ROI 3 that in other ROIs (Fig. 5). The participants who have read the IC with one page performed a more superficial reading in ROI 3 than participants that read ICs with two or three pages (Fig. 5).

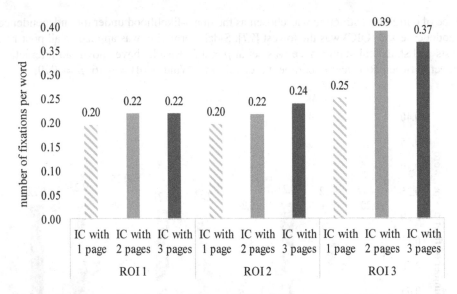

Fig. 5. Interaction effects between ROIs and IC length on reading depth in the last page

4 Discussion

The main goal of this study was to provide insights into the best standard for informed consent with eye tracking during the reading of a digital informed consent. The aim was thus to test whether reading depth changes throughout the reading of a digital informed consent with different lengths.

The results show a larger number of fixations per word at the bottom of the page (ROI 3) for participants that have read the shorter IC (IC with one page) when compared to participants that have read longer ICs (ICs with two and three pages). The number of fixations at the bottom of the one-page IC was higher, even when the comparisons were made for the first page and the last page of each condition. This result suggests that reading depth changes throughout reading the text of informed consent, possibly indicating that length influences the reading depth of such information.

A visual inspection of the figures suggests that the pattern of visual fixations is not so different between ROIs in each of the three length conditions. Interestingly, the reading depth (i.e. number of ocular fixations) increases from the top to the bottom on each length condition. Yet, this pattern is more consistent with the one-page condition. It is possible that the differences found on the first page between ICs lengths could be explained by a difference in the organization of the information. In the shorter IC condition, the information related to voluntary participation and the location of the participant signature was placed at the bottom of the first page, which may have captured more attention than the remaining sections. These results suggest increased attention allocation around the signature area, a section that may be used by clinicians and researchers to provide more complex information about the study, since participants' attention may be focused on this section more than on other sections of the IC.

More importantly, these results support the idea that when a participant reads an IC in digital format, s/he does not present a consistent reading depth along the page. Instead, participants tend to search for relevant verbal elements when they read which might be explained by the high number of fixations found at the bottom of the first page [28]. Surprisingly, the reading depth of the last page of the ICs was also lower at the top section of the page in comparison to the middle and bottom sections. These results suggest that people do a shallow reading of the contents at the top of the page. It is important to note that this pattern may have been motivated by the text headings, which depicted the most relevant contents and that should have been read more deeply [28, 29]. However, these results should be interpreted with caution given the study's limitations. A possible limitation of this study concerns the sequential mandatory reading in digital format which may have led to an artificial reading pattern. The participants that have read ICs with 2 or 3 pages were not able to read the previous page again. It would be important that future studies investigate the reading patterns in an IC presented in a paper sheet using eye tracking glasses, which would allow a more natural reading. In such setup, the use of regressive moves between pages as an index of involvement might help to get a deeper understanding of how participants read the IC. Future studies with this task using other eye tracking related data can also offer a different perspective to understand reading involvement and whether the participants are reading with critical analysis, for instance by pupil diameter as an index of cognitive effort [30]. Finally, the sample is a convenience sample of healthy participants without cognitive deficits, but future studies with clinical samples of patients with cognitive deficits due to different neurological conditions will be important to understand whether reading patterns of IC changes with cognitive function offer valuable insights into the relationship between high-order cognitive control processes and eye movements.

References

1. Mumford, M.: Psychology of the informed consent process: a commentary on three recent articles. Ethics Behav. 28(7), 513–516 (2018)
2. Pedersen, E., Neighbors, C., Tidwell, J., Lostutter, T.: Do undergraduate student research participants read psychological research consent forms? Examining memory effects, condition effects, and individual differences. Ethics Behav. 21(4), 332–350 (2011)
3. Ripley, K., Hance, M., Kerr, S., Brewer, L., Conlon, K.: Uninformed consent? The effect of participant characteristics and delivery format on informed consent. Ethics Behav. 28(7), 517–543 (2018)
4. Garrison, R., Eckstein, D.: Ethical considerations involving informed consent in Adlerian open forum counseling. J. Individ. Psychol. 69(4), 344–356 (2014)
5. Ilfeld, B.M.: Informed consent for medical research: an ethical imperative. Reg. Anesth. Pain Med. 31(4), 353–357 (2006)
6. Reamer, F.G.: Ethical issues in social work research. In: Thyer, B. (ed.) The Handbook of Social Work Research Methods, pp. 564–578. Sage Publications, Thousand Oaks (2010)
7. Sim, J., Dawson, A.: Informed consent and cluster-randomized trials, health policy and ethics. Am. J. Public Health 102(3), 480–485 (2012)

124   P. J. Rosa et al.

8. Tam, N., et al.: Participants' understanding of informed consent in clinical trials over three decades: systematic review and meta-analysis. Bull. World Health Organ. **93**, 186–198 (2015). https://doi.org/10.2471/BLT.14.141390
9. Grady, C.: Enduring and emerging challenges of informed consent. N. Engl. J. Med. **372**(9), 855–862 (2015). https://doi.org/10.1056/NEJMra1411250
10. Caplan, A.L.: Informed consent and provider-patient relationships in rehabilitation medicine. Arch. Phys. Med. Rehabil. **69**(5), 312–317 (2015)
11. Verástegui, E.L.: Consenting of the vulnerable: the informed consent procedure in advanced cancer patients in Mexico. BMC Med. Ethics **7**(13), 1–12 (2006)
12. Vossoughi, S.R., Macauley, R., Sazama, K., Fung, M.K.: Attitudes, practices, and training on informed consent for transfusions and procedures: a survey of medical students and physicians. Am. J. Clin. Pathol. **144**(2), 315–321 (2015). https://doi.org/10.1309/AJCPP85EXSGZORYZ
13. Johnson, M.L., Bellovin, S.M., Keromytis, A.D.: Computer security research with human subjects: risks, benefits and informed consent. In: Danezis, G., Dietrich, S., Sako, K. (eds.) FC 2011. LNCS, vol. 7126, pp. 131–137. Springer, Heidelberg (2012). https://doi.org/10.1007/978-3-642-29889-9_11
14. White, L.J., Jones, J.S., Felton, C.W., Pool, L.C.: Informed consent for medical research: common discrepancies and readability. Acad. Emerg. Med.: Off. J. Soc. Acad. Emerg. Med. **3**(8), 745–750 (1996)
15. Rayner, K., Slattery, T.J., Drieghe, D., Liversedge, S.P.: Eye movements and word skipping during reading: effects of word length and predictability. J. Exp. Psychol. Hum. Percept. Perform. **37**, 514–528 (2011)
16. Rosa, P.J., Esteves, F., Arriaga, P.: Effects of fear-relevant stimuli on attention: integrating gaze data with subliminal exposure. In: 2014 IEEE International Symposium on Medical Measurements and Applications (MeMeA), pp. 1–6 (2014). https://doi.org/10.1109/memea.2014.6860021
17. Rosa, P.J., Gamito, P., Oliveira, J., Morais, D., Pavlovic, M., Smyth, O.: Show me your eyes! The combined use of eye tracking and virtual reality applications for cognitive assessment. In: Fardoun, H.M., Gamito, P., Penichet, V.R., Alghazzawi, D.M. (eds.) Proceedings of the 2015 Workshop on ICTs for Improving Patients Rehabilitation Research Techniques (REHAB 2015), pp. 135–138. ACM, New York (2015). https://doi.org/10.1145/2838944.2838977
18. Rosa, P.J., Esteves, F., Arriaga, P.: Beyond traditional clinical measurements for screening fears and phobias. IEEE Trans. Instrum. Meas. **64**, 3396–3404 (2015). https://doi.org/10.1109/TIM.2015.2450292
19. Gamito, P., Oliveira, J., Baptista, A., et al.: Eliciting nicotine craving with virtual smoking cues. Cyberpsychology Behav. Soc. Netw. **17**(8), 556–561 (2014). https://doi.org/10.1089/cyber.2013.0329
20. Rosa, P.J., Lopes, P., Oliveira, J., Ambrósio, I., Silva., R.: Analog to digital: computerized application of Toulouse-Piéron combined with eye tracking. In: Fardoun, H.M., Penichet, V.R., Alghazzawi, D.M., Gamito, P. (eds.) Proceedings of the 4th Workshop on ICTs for Improving Patients Rehabilitation Research Techniques (REHAB 2016), pp. 69–72. ACM, New York (2016). https://doi.org/10.1145/3051488.3051507
21. Rosa, P.J., et al.: The effect of the number of pages on reading depth: preliminary contributions for a better-informed consent in neurorehabilitation. In: Fardoun, H.M., Penichet, V.R., Alghazzawi, D.M., Gamito, P. (eds.) Proceedings of the 4th Workshop on ICTs for improving Patients Rehabilitation Research Techniques (REHAB 2016), pp. 101–104. ACM, New York (2016). https://doi.org/10.1145/3051488.3051508

22. Holmqvist, K., Nyström, N., Andersson, R., Dewhurst, R., Jarodzka, H., van de Weijer, H.: Eye Tracking: A Comprehensive Guide to Methods and Measures. Oxford University Press, Oxford, New York (2011)

23. American Psychological Association: Ethical principles of psychologists and code of conduct. [Internet], January 2016. http://apa.org/ethics/code/index.aspx

24. Pichot, P., Brun, J.: Brief self-evaluation questionnaire for depressive, asthenic and anxious dimensions. Ann. Médico-psychologiques **142**(6), 862–865 (1984)

25. Rosa, P.J., Oliveira, J., Alghazzawi, D., Fardoun, H., Gamito, P.: Affective and physiological correlates of the perception of unimodal and bimodal emotional stimuli. Psicothema **29**(3), 364–369 (2017). https://doi.org/10.7334/psicothema2016.272

26. Rosa, P.J., Gamito, P., Oliveira, J., Morais, D., Pavlovic, M., Smyth, O.: Uso de eye tracking em realidade virtual não imersiva para avaliação cognitiva. Psicologia, Saúde & Doenças **17** (1), 23–31 (2016)

27. Cui, J., Qian, G.: Selection of working correlation structure and best model in GEE analyses of longitudinal data. Commun. Stat. – Simul. Comput. **36**(5), 987–996 (2007). https://doi.org/10.1080/03610910701539617

28. Davis, T.C., Holcombe, R.F., Berkel, H.J., Pramanik, S., Divers, S.G.: Informed consent for clinical trials: a comparative study of standard versus simplified forms. J. Natl. Cancer Inst. **90**(9), 668–674 (1998)

29. Rosa, P.J., Caires, C., Costa, L., Rodelo, L., Pinto, L.: Affective and psychophysiological responses to erotic stimuli: does color matter? In: Gamito, P., Rosa, P.J. (eds.) I See Me, You See Me: Inferring Cognitive and Emotional Processes From Gazing Behavior, pp. 171–190. Cambridge Scholars Publishing, Newcastle upon Tyne (2014)

30. van der Wel, P., van Steenbergen, H.: Pupil dilation as an index of effort in cognitive control tasks: a review. Psychon. Bull. Rev. https://doi.org/10.3758/s13423-018-1432-y. Epub ahead of print

How Usable Are Usability Tests? Examining the Suitability of Standard Usability Testing Methods for the Assessment of Apps for People Living with Dementia

Aideen Gibson[1] , Claire McCauley[1] ,
Maurice D. Mulvenna[2(✉)] , Assumpta Ryan[1] ,
Elizabeth A. Laird[1] , Kevin Curran[3] , Brendan Bunting[4] ,
Finola Ferry[5] , and Raymond Bond[2]

[1] School of Nursing, Ulster University, Londonderry BT48 7JL, UK
[2] School of Computing, Ulster University, Newtownabbey BT37 0QB, UK
md.mulvenna@ulster.ac.uk
[3] School of Computing, Engineering and Intelligent Systems, Ulster University,
Londonderry BT48 7JL, UK
[4] School of Psychology, Ulster University, Coleraine BT52 1SA, UK
[5] The Bamford Centre, Ulster University, Belfast BT15 1ED, UK

Abstract. The potential for technology to support memory or enhance cognition for people living with dementia is currently an area of significant interest. The use of digital systems to facilitate reminiscing has been shown to be beneficial for people living with dementia. This paper reports on a study that examines the value of several common usability testing protocols, methods and metrics when used to evaluate the usability of a new personalised reminiscence 'app' called 'InspireD'. InspireD is a bespoke app designed to support personalised reminiscence for people living with dementia. The app was co-created and designed with input from people living with dementia and their caregivers. The research question was 'are standard usability protocols appropriate to assess the usability of apps for individuals living with dementia?' The study aimed to determine on determining the appropriateness of methods commonly used to evaluate usability: concurrent think-aloud protocol; video recording and audio recording; metrics such as task completion rates; task completion times; single ease questions before and after task completion; and the systematic usability scale scores. Seven couples comprising a person with dementia with their primary caregiver evaluated the perceived usefulness and the level of user acceptance of the InspireD app. The study indicated that observation and recording of task completion rates and times produced the most reliable results, while the think-aloud methodology was difficult for the people living with dementia and did not produce any reliable data. Thinking-aloud whilst doing a task was perhaps a distraction since it requires a higher cognitive load. The systematic usability scale score which is derived from a post-test instrument is not reliable, as it had no association with the task completion times.

© Springer Nature Switzerland AG 2019
H. M. Fardoun et al. (Eds.): REHAB 2016, CCIS 1002, pp. 126–143, 2019.
https://doi.org/10.1007/978-3-030-16785-1_10

Keywords: Usability protocols · Usability · User experience · UX · Human computer interaction · User studies · Evaluation · Reminiscence · Apps · Assistive technology

1 Introduction

Dementia belongs to a range of progressive neurological condition, for which there is currently no cure. It is estimated that currently approximately 50 million people are living with dementia worldwide with 7.7 million new cases diagnosed every year [1]. It is estimated that in the UK there are 850,000 people living with a diagnosis of dementia [2].

As the disease progresses, mental processes are inhibited affecting memory, thinking, language, judgment, and it ultimately impacts an individual's ability to communicate. Dementia inhibits an individual's ability to present rational ideas and to reason lucidly [3]. However, it is now recognised that people living with dementia can become involved in research and provide invaluable feedback on Information Technology (IT) solutions [4].

Within UK Government policy, the development of new methods of care for those living with dementia has become a priority [5]. As the number of those living with dementia is continuing to rise the need for robust research, innovation and developments in non-pharmacological therapeutic interventions that provide immediate and accessible support to transform the delivery of care for those living with dementia and their family carers.

Reminiscence is an activity has the potential to enrich the lives of people living with dementia by sharing and reflecting of past memories which ware of personal significance to the individual. The act of reminiscing can be therapeutic in several ways by supporting the individual to reflect and to attribute meaning to special memories but can also create meaningful interactions between and individual and those closest to them [6]. A reminiscence system can therefore support the use of traditional prompts to evoke and stimulate memories and the feelings which underpin [7]. Reminiscence systems have been defined as 'the use of technology to support reminiscence work' [8]. Technology facilitated reminiscence can facilitate a readily accessible means of engagement for those living with dementia to play an active role in their conversations and social interactions [9].

There is currently a number of software applications and websites which offer the technological ability to browse, store and collate different media resources for an individual. However, for those experiencing cognitive decline there is very little research into how usable such systems are to facilitate reminiscence. In 2012, Thiry [10] proposed that social networking and online communities present a significant challenge for older people as they feel there is 'too much going on'. This work highlighted the need for system design that was 'simpler and minimalistic, offering only the most basic support for content creation and management'.

It is imperative and deemed good practice to involve all of the intended users of the technology in the design of the system [11, 12]. Therefore, industry standard measurements and protocols have been designed by human-computer-interaction researchers to ensure the usability of a system can be assessed [13, 14]. However, issues have been encountered when such standard usability protocols have been administered to a user group who is experiencing a decline in cognitive function and/or physical impairments [15]. Consideration may need to be given to the applicability of such generic usability measurements and how testing protocols which are suitable and reliable for different user groups could be designed.

As we move towards an inclusive society and the use of computer applications or 'apps' and ubiquitous devices become an integral part of everyday existence, there is an implicit need to design digital systems that can be used by all, regardless of their physical or cognitive abilities or impairments. It is therefore important that the design and development of digital systems and apps, whether these are general or specialist in purpose, should formally involve the intended target user group, and that usability protocols are suitable to evidence their contribution. This paper outlines the development and the assessment of usability of, a reminiscence system for people living with dementia, the InspireD app. It significantly expanded from an earlier workshop paper [16]. The paper proposes that in order to make user involvement a success there is a need to select traditional usability protocols carefully and tailor the evaluation/testing sessions to suit the target user group.

2 'InspireD' - A Reminiscence App

The size, capacity and low cost of ubiquitous devices and mobile tablet computers have made them an attractive option for designing and delivering reminiscence systems. As part of a feasibility study into the benefits of individual specific reminiscence, a cross-platform device agnostic tablet application (called InspireD) was developed to facilitate the activity of reminiscing for people with mild to moderate dementia. There were two aims in the development of the app, to enable those living with dementia and their family caregivers to select and store individual and specific memorabilia (photographs, videos, sounds, music) and to ensure the accessibility of these visual and audio-visual cues to facilitate personalised reminiscence.

The app consists of a user interface that is usable and responsive across a variety of mobile devices (tablets, mobile phones). It is also possible to use the system on a PC or laptop via the web browser. The main user (and co-users, i.e. caregivers) can upload images, video clips and audio clips to the app. SQLite database functionality is used to store and manage data natively. The main user interface consists of a simple screen for people living with dementia to upload files with help from a reminiscence trainer or a family caregiver. A multi-screen layout allows users to choose which memorabilia they wish to access, view photos, watch videos, or listen to audio files and browse selected resources (see Fig. 1).

InspireD was developed with input from the Reminiscence Network Northern Ireland and a 'lead user' couple which involved an individual living with dementia and their caregiver. An Agile software development approach [17] was adopted to allow a functional prototype to be created early in the development lifecycle, with testing and refinement taking place throughout the development process. The app was implemented using appcelerator Studio, an Eclipse-based IDE that provides an environment

Fig. 1. Sample screenshots of the InspireD reminiscence app user interface

to build, test, package, and publish apps for various platforms, including iOS and Android. The code is written in Javascript with native User Interface (UI) elements being invoked at runtime. It incorporates local facilities for persistent data storage in SQLite database and facilitates the use of 3rd party Application Programming Interfaces (API) for Flickr and YouTube (Fig. 2).

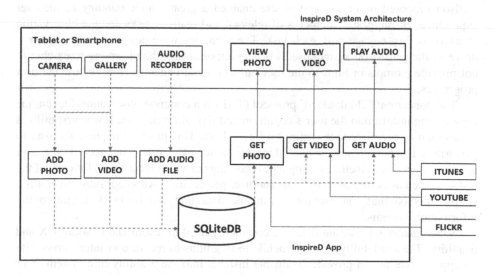

Fig. 2. InspireD app – system architecture

The design is minimalist, using verbal descriptors as well as images and icons to reinforce and indicate functionality to the user. Data is organised and presented primarily in the form of on-screen menus. The welcome screen is a simple login screen where the user confirms their identity by clicking a photo of themselves.

The user data is contained within a local SQLite database, which can be easily queried with reporting services enabled. Multimedia reminiscing resources (photos/videos/audios) are also stored locally in the app data directory. The system was designed with scalability in mind for future enhancements as it is envisaged that the final version will be a secure, cloud-based application, where data will be accessible via a secure Internet connection for authorized users.

3   Evaluating Usability

The evaluation of usability is based on how easily a system can achieve its intended goals and the efficiency of user interaction with the system through its user interface. Usability has been defined by Nielson as, 'a quality attribute that assesses how easy user interfaces are to use' [18]. Standard measurements to assess these attributes can be involve: observation; concurrent thinking-aloud; single ease questions; recording by video and/or audio; and the post-test survey, the systematic usability scale. The metrics produced by these methods can be are used by researchers to determine the usability of the user interface.

3.1   Observational Approaches

Neilson proposed observing system use enabled a greater understanding of the user experience. He suggested a process of relevant and realistic tasks and the observation of users as they engage with each task. The scenarios were designed to be representative of the real world system use. It is also important for the observing researcher to not provide prompts or hints to the user but to instead patiently observe how the user progresses.

The concurrent 'Think-aloud' protocol (TAP) is a common observational technique for eliciting insight into the user's cognition and thought processes. It was first utilised for evaluating user interface design by Lewis [19]. This protocol requires the user to perform a number of tasks while 'thinking aloud'. The researcher records the user actions (written or sometimes using tape recordings or video recordings) for each of the tasks, as well as noting any problems and user perplexities. Although subjective, it is a simple method that can provide a valuable data that can be used for improving information systems.

Video analysis recording (REC) is commonly used to record and measure UX and usability. The availability of small mobile testing units to record user interactions with an app or website can provide invaluable insights into the usability of a system. This moderated 'lab' usability testing scenario is still one of the best ways to capture the rich experience of interacting with a mobile device [20]. It allows researchers to capture the rich interactions between the user and the device as well as any verbalisation from 'thinking-aloud'. Video analysis also allows for detailed event annotations, frequency of use errors and the use of timestamps to measure task completion times. Very often, the web cam is also recorded to detect any user frustration with the interface.

3.2 Questionnaire-Based Approaches

The Single Ease Question (SEQ) is a 7-point rating scale to assess how difficult users find a task [21]. The user estimates the level of difficulty before and after attempting the task, using the 7-point rating scale. The validity of the measurement is greater as it is recorded immediately after each task is attempted rather than at the end of the session.

The systematic usability scale (SUS) is a post-test survey, has become an industry standard questionnaire for measuring the usability of a system [22]. The SUS scale consists of 10 questions with response options presented in a Likert scale format. Each question has 5 possible responses (between 1 and 5 where 5 = strongly agree). This scale is a well-balanced instrument as half of the questions have positive connotations and five are more negatively focused. All SUS scale responses are then converted to a systematic usability scale score (or SUS score) and the mean value is then used to indicate system usability. The mean SUS score is calculated using the formulae presented in Eq. 1 below.

$$\overline{SUS} = \frac{1}{n}\sum\nolimits_{i=1}^{n} norm \cdot \sum\nolimits_{j=1}^{m} \begin{cases} q_{i,j} - 1, & q_{i,j} \bmod 2 > 0 \\ 5 - q_{i,j}, & otherwise. \end{cases} \tag{1}$$

where n is the number of subjects, m is the number of questions (m = 10) and $q_{i,j}$ is a rating from one question by one subject (whilst norm = 2.5 in order to provide a normalised ratio or score out of 100). A mean SUS score greater than 68 is considered above average since this is the accepted mean SUS score from a distribution of SUS scores previously collected from usability tests.

The usability phase of the system development lifecycle often assumes a high level of cognitive ability and communication on the part of the users. When developing a system to support reminiscing it is important to choose appropriate methodologies and protocols to test the usability of the system. This research paper describes the usability protocols selected to assess usability of the InspireD app. The value of these protocols to measure the usability of the InspireD app is qualitatively examined. The suitability of each protocol to assess the usability of an app by people living with dementia is discussed.

3.3 Task Completion-Based Approaches

Task completion rate (TCR) is a percentage measure of users who completed the task [23]. When determining the usability of s system, task completion is probably the most important measure, for example, if a user cannot complete a designated task when engaging with the system, it is deemed a poorly designed system. Thus, the objective of any system design if to achieve a 100% task completion rate which would indicate its use is intuitive for the intended user. The inverse of this measurement is the task failure rate.

Task completion time (TCT) is a metric which reveals the amount of time a user requires to complete a specified task [23]. Within usability testing the mean task completion time is often referred to as a key usability metric. However, the geometric mean task completion time should be calculated for smaller datasets. Nevertheless, the mean task completion time can be compared to the expert task completion time, which will indicate the gap between expert and novice performance. An additional measurement is the time-until failure, which is representative of the time a user is willing to commit to completing the designated task before giving up.

4 Study Design

This study aimed to investigate the suitability of standard usability protocols for the use of a reminiscence app by those living with dementia and their caregiver. Seven dyads, each comprising a person living with dementia and their caregiver worked with researchers to investigate the appropriateness, validity and reliability of several standard usability tests and matrices. The measurements used for investigation in this study includes the following:

- Concurrent think-aloud protocol (TAP) [19];
- Video recording and audio recording devices (REC) [20];
- Task completion rates (TCR) [23];
- Task completion times (TCT) [23];
- Single Ease Questions (SEQ) [21]; and
- Systematic Usability Scale (SUS) [22].

The measurements recorded were examined and discussed with the participating dyads in a series of five workshops during a 6-week period. The study received full ethical approval from Ulster University's Research Ethics Committee study (Fig. 3).

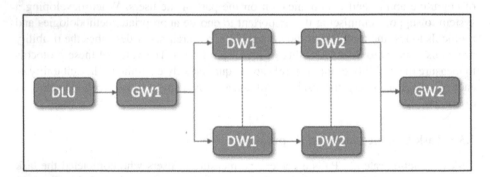

Fig. 3. Sequence of planned workshops (See Sect. 5 for explanation of acronyms)

The first workshop consisted of a pilot test which was conducted with the lead user dyad to identify any potential issues or barriers that would arise for people living with dementia when testing the app. The subsequent "usability workshops" were carried out with the 6 other testing couples over a period of 4 weeks.

5 Experiments

A user development group was formed to test the usability of the reminiscence system by those living with dementia and their carers. The user development group included 7 adults living with dementia (5 men and 2 women) and 7 caregivers (all women), with an age range (n = 14) was 42–77. One dyad, referred to as the lead user dyad (LU), was involved in the preliminary stages of the research study to inform the design of app development. The remaining user dyads were recruited from the Alzheimer's Society Home Support Network. Those interested in participating were provided with detailed information and the opportunity to clarify their contribution to the planned workshops and to discuss any concerns about study involvement with the researchers, before informed consent was obtained.

The first workshop (DLU) involved a pilot test of the system prototype in the home of the lead user dyad to identify any potential issues or challenges when testing the app for people living with dementia. The following 4 usability workshops were conducted with the remaining six dyads over a period of 6 weeks. Two of the four workshops (GW1 and GW2) were conducted as group sessions in the university campus, while the other two workshops (DW1 and DW2) were delivered as an individual intervention in the dyads home. Within the time period of DW1 and DW2 the dyads tested the usability of the app during 1–2 weeks of home use.

5.1 Preparation

The first (GW1) and last (GW2) group workshops were conducted in the form of an introductory group meeting and a final focus group, respectively. Suitable dates and times were arranged with the group and a dementia friendly venue on the university campus was used for both workshops. The dyad usability workshops (DW) took place in the home of the person living with dementia in the form of semi-structured interviews with each individual in each set of dyads. It was decided that two researchers would be present at all of the workshops to record notes and to document the interviews.

Information leaflets and consent forms were prepared for both the people living with dementia and their caregivers, to be distributed at the first workshop. A pre-test questionnaire was designed to determine the participants' previous IT experience and device usage. Notes were prepared for the participants on how to turn on, login, and initiate the iPad. They were also shown how to do simple tasks such as launch an app or change the audio volume on the device.

The iPads were set up using standard settings with screen rotation and password protection enabled and no special accessibility settings were used. Excluding the camera icon and the Safari icon, all other standard icons which normally appear on the home screen were organised and put into the Extras folder, so that the users would not be distracted. The side switch was also set to lock the orientation of the user interface and auto-lock was extended to 15 min. Siri was switched off and auto complete was switched on. Brightness was set to approx. 75% and auto-brightness was enabled. The standard wallpaper was used for GW1. For the individual workshops, the InspireD app was installed on the iPad and the icon was placed in the bottom toolbar beside Safari. The wallpaper was changed to a light blue still for these workshops (DW1, DW2).

During each of the two usability workshops (DW1, DW2) conducted in the homes of participating dyads, each individual living with dementia and each caregiver was asked to conduct a number of tasks related to app use under the observation of researchers who recorded notes (Table 1). These tasks, described below, were scheduled to be completed on two separate occasions with each person being observed for around thirty minutes. It was planned that the first set of tasks would be recorded using an audio recording device and the second set of tasks would be recorded using a video recording camera.

Table 1. Tasks observed in DW1 and DW2

Task description	Completed	Ref
Select a photo from personal collection and make it full size	Individually	DW1
Go back to photo collections, scroll through, find steam engine and select	Individually	DW1
Go back to home screen. Select video of Gerry Anderson and play	Individually	DW1
Stop the video and go back to home	Individually	DW1
Open Music folder and find the song by The Beach Boys	Individually	DW1
Go back to the Home screen and Exit the app	Individually	DW1
Add a new user: name and photo	As a dyad	DW2
Upload a photo to the app and add tags and a description	As a dyad	DW2
Upload a photo to the app and add a short narrative	As a dyad	DW2
Take a picture of an object and save it to the app	As a dyad	DW2
Add a video to the app	As a dyad	DW2
Add a sound clip to the app	As a dyad	DW2

In the design of DW1 and DW2, twelve typical tasks were identified for the users to complete. These tasks were specifically devised so they would be realistic, actionable and avoid unnecessary prompting from the research team or the carer. The DW1 tasks involved using the app to conduct basic reminiscing – engaging with photographs, watching movie clips and listening to audio clips. The DW2 tasks were related to selecting, uploading and recording reminiscing materials to the app.

A task completion grid was printed for the researchers to record the metrics for time taken by each participant to complete each task. The single ease question scale was used to record and assess how difficult users found each task. An audio recording device and video recording software and hardware (point-to-view) were selected to video record the tasks and the verbalisation of the think-aloud data. The device used is called Mobile Observation Device (or MOD-1000) which is a popular mobile testing unit [20]. A post-test SUS questionnaire was designed to obtain feedback on the users' perception of the app to be administered at the final focus group.

Table 2 illustrates the different usability measurements conducted with the lead user dyad (DLU), group workshops (GWn) and dyad workshops (DWn). The following sub-sections outline the usability testing conducted with the User Development Group.

Table 2. Engagement matrix with usability measures

	DLU	GW1	DW1	DW2	GW2
TAP	✓		✓	✓	
REC			✓	✓	
TCR			✓	✓	
TCT				✓	
SEQ		✓			
SUS					✓

5.2   Lead User Dyad Workshop (DLU)

The lead user dyad included an adult male living with dementia who will be designated the pseudonym 'Mike' and his female carer. 'Mike' was aged 42 years of age at the time of involvement, he had a high level of computing competence and already had compiled his own collections of digital photographs, videos and music.

During a one hour session both individuals tested the app to identify if there were any potential barriers that would prevent those living with dementia from contributing to the usability workshops. 'Mike' was asked to carry out designated tasks, these app interactions were then observed and recorded by the researchers to inform the protocol for the user development workshops. The carers views and opinions were also recorded to guide the planning and preparation of the workshops for the user development group.

A form of usability testing which consisted of 'think-aloud' task analysis enabled the LU to describe what they were doing and their thought processes behind their interaction. The researchers asked 'Mike' to comment on the sound and the user interface image quality, display and size of text. Additional feedback was sought regarding button size with specific reference to the help and exit buttons. Researchers recorded their observations on how easy or how difficult 'Mike' found interactions with the touchscreen device. The LU identified no obvious barriers to those living with dementia being centrally involved in testing the app.

5.3   First Group Workshop (GW1)

It is Sauro and Lewis's [23] view the experience of usage is more impactful on usability measurements than demographics. Accordingly, in the first group workshop GW1 all user dyads were introduced to the basic functioning of the tablet (iPad) to minimise an potential for digital literacy bias. In the first workshop user dyads were not introduced to the InspireD app to ensure this did not impact their ability to conduct the specific usability tests in the home based workshops in DW1 and DW2.

The session began with introductions, subsequently researchers explained the aims of GW1 and its significance within at this developmental stage in the research study. Informed consent forms was obtained participant questions were addressed. A pre-test questionnaire was completed by all the participants to determine their previous experience and use of IT systems.

The researchers provided verbal instructions as to how to turn on an iPad, launch an app (Safari), close the app and turn the device off. Researchers then asked participants to look at generic photographs on Flickr and participants were shown how to 'swipe' between screen pages.

5.4   First Dyad Workshop (DW1)

This workshop was conducted in the homes of each dyad. The purpose of this session was to access was the usability of the InspireD app was at facilitating reminiscing. Both the person living with dementia and their family carer were asked to complete the same task and the completion rates and completion times for each task was recorded.

All of the six tasks which were to be completed were related to the use of the app as an aid for reminiscing. These tasks including looking at generic photographs, watching. The tasks involved looking at photographs, watching videos clips and listening to audio files. The participants rated the level of difficulty of each task using SEQ before and after each attempt, which was recorded by the researchers.

5.5   Second Dyad Workshop (DW2)

The second home-based usability workshop aimed to evaluate two key aspects of usage, the addition of different users to the system and the ease of uploading material to facilitate reminiscence, e.g., photographs, videos and music. In this session the completion rates and times of each task were recorded. A mobile observation device (MOD-1000, a USB macro camera) was used to record the image of the dyads tablet during the session and researchers made additional interview notes. The observation device is designed to be as unobtrusive as possible, it is mounted on an aluminium plate with a non-slip surface. One researcher recorded the task completed grid the second researcher made dyad specific observations. As before the SEQ was used before and after each task attempt to estimate the level of difficulty which was recorded on the response grid.

5.6   Second Group Workshop (GW2)

Following a period of home use for 1–2 weeks, the user development group meet as a group for the final session which was conducted as a focus group within the university to assess the user experience of the app. Within this group session participants were asked to complete the SUS survey to assess the user developments groups views on the usability of the app. All focus group feedback was recorded using an audio recording device and was transcribed to enable a detailed evaluation of how satisfied the user was with the app.

Table 3. Overview of clustered themes and sub-categories gathered from GW2

Clusters and sub-categories of issues compiled after analysis of results		
Theme	Sub-categories	Issue
Interaction with app	General look and feel Font – colours, size System messages Button size	Exit button (Video) Stop button Could not read system message for recording video Pressed audio image to play song
Manage screen	System functionality – separating adding resources and browsing resources	Too complicated, not intuitive
Hardware/software	Swiping left and right Physical product Physical buttons Increasing sound	Difficulty with 'swipe' action Difficult to increase volume using buttons
Condition specific	Semantics Colours/icons Components outside of their periphery of vision	Help button (Suggested information) Placement of exit Button (System)/Back buttons
Other	Opportunities Methods	Fewer stylised icons Fewer components on each screen

Table 3 provides an overview of the identified clustered themes and sub-categories gathered from this workshop.

6 Results

The DLU testing of the touch screen device identified no obvious barriers which could prevent those living with dementia from engaging in the testing phase of the app. The image quality, display and size of the text and sound quality of the touch screen interface on the device were all deemed satisfactory by the DLU. However, some issues while most screen buttons were easy to use, both the Help and Exit buttons were problematic in relation to their positioning on the screen interface.

Mike was able to navigate the app and complete 5/6 tasks. Both this person with dementia and their caregiver were in agreement with the use of colours and size of the main buttons and agreed that the icons were appropriate. They agreed that the text in some of the messages displayed by the system was too small and difficult to read.

The 'thinking aloud' presented some difficulties for 'Mike' as he, at times, strayed off topic and had difficulty describing his actions and explaining his thought processes while carrying out the tasks. As a result, 'Mike's' carer had to intervene to help focus him back to the specific task and towards the app. His caregiver had to bring him back to the actual task and steer the conversation towards the app.

6.1   General Findings

The group and data workshop data were analysed in a similar participatory approach to that used of Brankaert et al. [24].

In the first group workshop (GW1), a typical user profile was established for the participants. Five of the 6 people living with dementia were male, with all of the caregivers being female. They ranged in age from 55 to 77 and there was a very wide-ranging spectrum of user experience of IT and use of technology. One-third of the participants had never used a computer. Two-thirds of the participants have used a touch screen device in the past (this included touch screen tills in supermarkets and cash machines). Only half of the participants have used audio devices like an iPod to listen to music and fewer than half have access to a tablet device at home. However, 11/12 of the participants have experience of using a mobile phone. Three of the people living with dementia quickly learned how to use the device and they said they had 'no difficulty' using the iPad. Two of the people living with dementia were comfortably able to carry out the tasks with simple instructions from their caregiver. One person found it very difficult to press the buttons. Five of the 6 caregivers had no difficulty using the iPad, while one caregiver was confident using it with help from the person with dementia. Both the person with dementia and their caregiver were comfortable using the app and completed all of the tasks described in Table 1 without additional support from the researcher. Some prompts from the caregiver were given to the person with dementia to keep them focused on the task in hand but no significant issues were identified during this session that would indicate that people living with dementia would be unable to participate in the testing of the app.

In the first dyad workshop, researchers observed that each carer could confidently use the app when using it to engage with reminiscence material evidenced by their 100% task completion rate. The second task which involved scrolling through a group of images was challenging for all but one of the individuals living with dementia. Task 6, which involved going back to the previous screen and exiting the app presented a difficulty for all but two of the participants living with dementia. The remaining four tasks were completed by no less that three of the participants living with dementia. However, one of the individuals living with dementia was unable to complete any of the tasks. In the second dyad workshop, 96% of the tasks were successfully completed as carried out as a dyad (which included the person living with dementia and their carer due to a mutually supportive approach.

The researchers piloted the think-aloud protocol with the DLU as it had envisaged that this would reveal the thought process involved in the user experience. However, it became evident in both the DLU and in the user development group workshops that participants living with dementia had significant difficulty verbalising what they were thinking even if they were frequently prompted or reminded by their carer to do so when completing the tasks.

In the second dyad workshop, the MOD-1000 mobile observation device was introduced to record the tablet when the participant was engaging with it. It was intended that the mobile device would record the uploading of materials to the app by each dyad. When observing participant interactions, it became apparent to the researchers that the device was distracting and confusing, interfering with the completion go each specified task. Mobile observation is a standard usability protocol, however, participants living with dementia confused the mobile observation device as part of the reminiscence system. Consequently, it was decided by the research team to no longer include the mobile camera device in the following workshops.

In the second dyad workshop researcher noted differing task completion times, which varied depending on the age and previous experience of the participants. The researchers estimated that the completion of all 6 tasks would take 30 min. One participant, who identified himself as having IT experience took 25 min to complete all 6 tasks, in comparison to 34, the slowest rate of completion.

The second dyad workshop was completed by each dyad as a mutually supportive pair, as the difficulty ratings in the 6 tasks completed were recorded and analysed (see Table 4).

Table 4. Results of SEQ for DW2

Task	Expected difficulty rating (edr)	Actual difficulty rating (adr)	Delta (edr - adr)	p-values
1	4.17 (2.93)	3.00	−0.03	0.59
2	3.50 (2.88)	3.67	−1.02	0.92
3	3.33 (2.94)	2.67	−2.13	0.59
4	3.67 (2.58)	2.83	−1.25	0.86
5	2.33 (1.03)	2.67	0.33	0.58
6	3.50 (2.43)	3.83	0.05	0.47

A negative Delta value suggests the task was easier than anticipated, while a positive value means it was harder than expected by the user group. While the results from this study would indicate that participants found the tasks to be easier than they had anticipated, however, given the small number of users tested in this study the results would be insignificant (see p-values in Table 4).

When measuring participant perceptions of usability, the systematic usability scale has become an industry standard questionnaire for post-test survey. Caregivers gave the InspireD app a mean rating of 67.5% (SD = 11.55) while the SUS questionnaire completed by 4 people living with dementia awarded the app 78.75%. As a mean SUS score greater than 68 is considered above average, therefore, results indicate that the app is usable [22]. However, analysis of the task completion rates (TCR) would suggest the app was more easily used by the carers than the participants living with dementia. The reliability and validity of the SUS scale as a measure of usability, is questionable in this user group. A possible explanation of could be that participants living with dementia and their carers had differing perceptions of task difficulty. Those living with dementia indicated that they found the app enjoyable to use and would recommend its use to a friend as a pleasure experience. However, it is plausible that the SUS questions were difficult to understand or their short term recall was limited and they could not remember the difficulties experienced when using the app or completing the tasks. As short – term memory is directly affected by dementia, this has implications for future research involving those living with dementia.

7 Discussion

The results from this study revealed that the most reliable results were obtained from observation and recording of task completion rates as, while the think-aloud methodology was very difficult for people living with dementia and did not produce any reliable data (Table 5).

Table 5. Summary of findings on the suitability of usability measures

	Summary of findings
TAP	Requires intensive facilitator and/or caregiver interaction and management, supporting prospective memory of person living with dementia
REC	The MOD-1000 camera device was removed as it was found to distracted users when they were completing assigned tasks. In addition, it was perceived by the users to be an additional component of the reminiscence device
TCR	This was found to be a reliable usability metric for all usability tests independent of user profile
TCT	This was found to be a reliable usability metric for all usability tests independent of user profile
SEQ	Not useful for people living with dementia as they find it difficult to estimate how difficult a task should be, perhaps exposing a lack of experience with digital technology
SUS	The SUS was an invalid instrument in this study. The scores from users living with dementia were not reliable, as they did not concur with task completion rates. This may be because any post-test survey relies on reflection and short term memory. An additional challenge presented to users living with dementia, is alternating negatively and positively worded questions

Participants living with dementia also experienced difficulties assigning a numerical value in the SEQ pre and post task evaluation. Only caregivers were able to assign reliable difficulty rating to the questions as participants living with dementia found it confusing to assign a number to a perceived difficulty rating. The completion of post-test questionnaires administered to participants living with dementia after an event was challenging, once again indicating the impact of short-term memory loss. As a result, the SUS scores reliability could not be guaranteed. The InspireD app had an overall SUS rating of 67.5% by carers but 78.75% by the 4 participants living with dementia who completed the questionnaire. However, it is noteworthy that the task completion rates revealed caregivers found it easier to use the app, than people living with dementia.

Caregivers completion rates were significantly higher than those living with dementia, with 100% of tasks successfully in the GW1 and 96% of the tasks they were set in GW2. Of the participants living with dementia, the 5 individuals who were able to complete some of the tasks without prompts or support had much lower completion rates than their carers. In general, the SUS instrument can be present difficulties as post-test surveys requires accurate retrospective reflection in the user experience. The SUS survey design is intricate in which the Likert scale of each question interchanges the highest rating as positive and negative feedback. The usability evaluations identified a total of 10 consistent errors/usability issues which were noted by the researchers observing the participants using the system and were confirmed by the completion rates and the focus group.

A number of factors could have affected the results of the usability tests, including the usability protocols selected, the venue choice to conduct the testing and the time given to allow participants to feel comfortable.

The aim of this research study was to assess if standard tests and matrices were appropriate for those with cognitive impairment to evaluate the usability of the InspireD app. The protocols which were contingent on thinking and reasoning functions in the brain and involved estimations of levels of difficulty or process descriptions such as thinking aloud were particularly problematic for users living with dementia and experiencing short-term memory loss.

All of the user development group dyads remained with the study until it was completed, although 1 female person with dementia and their caregiver was unable to attend the final focus group. As was expected, most of the caregivers (n = 5) found it considerably easier to use the application than the people living with dementia. This was evident from observation and analysis of task completion rates. However, this did not concur with the SUS scores when they were examined.

Of the 4 people living with dementia who did complete the questionnaires, their answers did not correlate directly to their actual observed experience of using the app. Two out of the six people living with dementia were unable to complete SUS as they could not understand the questions sufficiently or remember their experience of using the app. Data collection should focus on understanding errors related to accessibility rather than time on task or user satisfaction.

8 Conclusion

The InspireD app was designed and developed with input from a lead user couple and the Reminiscence Network NI. Standard usability measurements and protocols were used to test the app, designed to facilitate the process of reminiscence, by those living with dementia and their family caregiver over a 6-week testing period. It is widely accepted that user involvement in design and testing of IT systems is necessary. As more apps and medical technologies are being developed for use by people living with dementia, it is becoming necessary to adapt and refine traditional research methodologies to effectively evaluate the usability of these applications.

Our results and observations would indicate that the use of the SUS post-test survey may not be a suitable measure of user experience when administered to those living with a condition that impacts their short term. In addition, researchers identified challenges when using the mobile usability testing unit (MOD 1000: Mobile Observation Device) as users were confusing the attached camera with the tablet under testing. As those living with dementia have difficulties verbalising their though processes, audio recording were unnecessary as no 'think-aloud' data on their human-computer interaction was recorded. Our conclusion is that for those living with dementia, standard usability metrics to test IT systems and applications are not sensitive too or suitable for capturing their contribution to IT design. It is equally important to assess the appropriateness of the metrics we use to assess usability as it is to consider the news of the intended user group when designing the system.

In conclusion, our results suggest that the InspireD mobile app is usable for the small sample size of those living with dementia. Our research indicated that the app is easy to use for people who are not living with dementia and could support those living with dementia to use the app for the purposes of reminiscence. The results would further indicate that industry standard common usability testing protocols which include the SUS instrument, think-aloud protocols and the mobile macro cameras attached to the device are not appropriate to assess the usability of apps designed for user groups who are living with conditions causing progressive cognitive decline such as dementia. This suggests that further research is required to design new protocols or to amend existing usability metrics to improve the data generated from the testing of devices and apps in these contexts.

Acknowledgments. The authors would like to acknowledge the invaluable contribution to the co-created and design of the reminiscence app from the Alzheimer's Society, Reminiscence Network Northern Ireland (RNNI) and the User Development Group members. Additional thanks to Alex Turnbull, Software Engineer from Kainos Software Limited for the specialist and invaluable assistance in decisions around technology selection. The funding support provided by HSC R&D Grant COM/5016/14 "A feasibility study of facilitated reminiscence for people with dementia" is gratefully acknowledged by the authors.

References

1. WHO Dementia Factsheet. http://www.who.int/mediacentre/factsheets/fs362/en/. Accessed 11 May 2016
2. Alzheimer's Society: Dementia 2014 report statistics. https://www.alzheimers.org.uk/site/scripts/documents_info.php?documentID=341. Accessed 11 May 2016
3. NHS: Communicating with people with dementia. http://www.nhs.uk/conditions/dementia-guide/pages/dementia-and-communication.aspx. Accessed 11 May 2016
4. Span, M., Hettinga, M., Vernooij-Dassen, M., Eefsting, J., Smits, C.: Involving people with dementia in the development of supportive IT applications: a systematic review. Ageing Res. Rev. **12**(2), 535–551 (2013). https://doi.org/10.1016/j.arr.2013.01.002
5. Prime Minister's Challenge on Dementia 2020: Department of Health, February 2015
6. Butler, R.N.: The life review: an interpretation of reminiscence in the aged. Psychiatry **26**, 65–76 (1963)
7. Gibson, F.: Reminiscence and Life Story Work: A Practice Guide. Jessica Kingsley Publishers, London (2011)

8. Mulvenna, M.D., Astell, A.J., Zheng, H., Wright, T.: Reminiscence systems. In: Mulvenna, M.D., Astell, A.J., Zheng, H., Wright, T., (eds.) Proceedings of First International Workshop on Reminiscence Systems, Cambridge, UK, September 2009, pp. 2–4 (2009)
9. Lazar, A., Thompson, H., Demiris, G.: A systematic review of the use of technology for reminiscence therapy. Health Educ. Behav. **41**, 51S–61S (2014). https://doi.org/10.1177/1090198114537067
10. Thiry, E.: Designing a digital reminiscing system for older adults. SIGACCESS Access. Comput. **105**, 24–28 (2013). https://doi.org/10.1145/2444800.2444805
11. Carroll, J.M., Rosson, M.B.: Participatory design in community informatics. Des. Stud. **28** (3), 243–261 (2007)
12. Muller, M.J.: Participatory design: the third space in HCI. Hum.-Comput. Interact. Handb. **4235**(6), 1051–1068 (2002)
13. Lewis, J.R.: Usability Testing: Handbook of Human Factors and Ergonomics, 3rd edn, pp. 1275–1316. Wiley, Hoboken (2006)
14. Sauro, J.: 10 Essential Usability Metrics. https://measuringu.com/essential-metrics/. Accessed 30 Aug 2018
15. Astell, A., Alm, N., Gowans, G., Ellis, M., Dye, R., Vaughan, P.: Involving older people with dementia and their carers in designing computer based support systems – some methodological considerations. Univers. Access Inf. Soc. **8**, 49–58 (2009)
16. Gibson, A., et al.: Assessing usability testing for people living with dementia. In: Fardoun, H.M., Penichet, V.R., Alghazzawi, D.M., Gamito, P. (eds.) Proceedings of the 4th Workshop on ICTs for Improving Patients Rehabilitation Research Techniques, REHAB 2016, pp. 25–31. ACM, New York (2016). https://doi.org/10.1145/3051488.3051492
17. Aydin, M.N., Harmsen, F., van Slooten, K., Stegwee, R.A.: On the adaptation of an agile information systems development method. J. Database Manag. Spec. Issue Agile Anal. Des. Implement. **16**(4), 20–24 (2005). https://doi.org/10.4018/jdm.2005100102
18. Nielsen, J.: Usability Engineering, 1st edn. Academic Press, London (1993)
19. Lewis, C.: Using the 'thinking-aloud' method in cognitive interface design. (IBM Research Report RC 9265, 2/17/82). IBM T.J. Watson Research Center, Yorktown Heights (1982)
20. Sauro, J.: How to conduct a usability test on a mobile device. https://measuringu.com/mobile-usability-test/. Accessed 30 Aug 2018
21. Sauro, J., Dumas, J.S.: Comparison of three one-question, post-task usability questionnaires. In: Proceedings of the SIGCHI Conference on Human Factors in Computing Systems, CHI 2009, pp. 1599–1608. ACM, New York (2009). http://dx.doi.org/10.1145/1518701.1518946
22. Bangor, A., Kortum, P.T., Miller, J.T.: An empirical evaluation of the system usability scale. Int. J. Hum. Comput. Interact. **24**(6), 574–594 (2008)
23. Sauro, J., Lewis, J.R.: Quantifying the User Experience: Practical Statistics for User Research. Elseiver, Amsterdam (2012). Accessed Mar 2016
24. Brankaert, R., Ouden, E.D.: (Re) Design of a mobile interface: reflections on an in-context evaluation. In: Proceedings of Participatory Innovation Conference 2015, The Hague, The Netherlands (2015)

Author Index

Printed in the United States
By Bookmasters